Endorsements

These short stories describe in a very beautiful and human way the mystery of the gospels. Never before have I been so helped in my faith journey by such stories of doubt, hope, wondering, uncertainty, obeying without knowing, sheer humanity, serendipitous moments, and different characters used by God to fulfill his plans.

Reading these stories brought something very grounded in the real world of living for me. I would recommend that others living in the chaos of uncertainty on their faith journey read and be inspired and encouraged by these stories.

—Olive Hobson
Northern Ireland

The most significant bridge across time and history is the story. How better to understand and appreciate the power of the gospels than to hear them told by a master storyteller. These stories come alive as told through that rare combination of an academic's mind and a pastor's heart.

Dr. James E Brenneman
President, Goshen College, Goshen IN.

In *Meeting Jesus* Don Blosser has crafted a rich anthology of common folks and their uncommon encounters with Jesus.

These vignettes reach far beyond the days of the New Testament. They awaken our interest in familiar biblical texts and inspire us as we ponder our own meetings with those who reflect the Light of Christ. These stories are well suited for use in small groups and worship settings. As we read, may we marvel at Jesus' love for the ordinary and find ourselves among these pages.

—Anita Rediger
Pastor, Emmaus Road Mennonite Fellowship, Berne, IN.

Written in first person and using fresh, modern language, these stories bring ancient texts to life. They open new insights and emotions through imagination and inspiration. I hear them as testimonies or monologues that could be used in worship or in Sunday school classes for youth or adults.

—Don Yost
Founder, Bridgework Theater, Communications Director
Maple City Health Center, Goshen, IN.

i

Also written by Don Blosser:

Pastor and Professor: A Public Faith 2012

To Continue the Dialogue (contributor) 2001

Jesus: His Life and Times (contributor) 1998

Dictionary of the Literature of the Bible 1996

The Coming Kingdom 1982

Meeting Jesus

Common People. . .Uncommon Stories

Benton Mennonite Church

May you also tell your own story

Don Blosser

Donald Blosser

WESTBOW·
PRESS
A DIVISION OF THOMAS NELSON
& ZONDERVAN

Cathy Hagen – Artist

New Revised Standard Version Bible, copyright © 1989, Division of Christian
Education of the National Council of the Churches of Christ in the United
States of America. Used by permission. All rights reserved.

*This is a work of fiction. All of the characters, names, incidents, organizations, and dialogue
in this novel are either the products of the author's imagination or are used fictitiously.*

WestBow Press books may be ordered through booksellers or by contacting:

WestBow Press
A Division of Thomas Nelson & Zondervan
1663 Liberty Drive
Bloomington, IN 47403
www.westbowpress.com
1 (866) 928-1240

ISBN: 978-1-4908-7539-2 (sc)
ISBN: 978-1-4908-7541-5 (hc)
ISBN: 978-1-4908-7540-8 (e)

Library of Congress Control Number: 2015905180

Print information available on the last page.

WestBow Press rev. date: 04/06/2015

Contents

Dedication

Meeting Jesus: Common People ... Uncommon Stories is dedicated to the memory of Magdalene Liechty ("Maggie" to everyone who knew her). She was constantly exploring the edges of her faith and asking questions without accepting any easy answers. Maggie's health placed severe restrictions on her movement and social interaction, but her mind accepted no limitations. She wanted to explore ideas, and she made quick connections. She had a faith that was passionate while expecting integrity; she was profoundly spiritual while being practical and realistic.

Maggie died August 13, 2014. We had said our good-byes with mixed emotions. It was right that she go, but neither of us was done yet. During her lifetime, she would have objected, but now I can say it: "Maggie, you truly were one of God's saints among us. My life was richly blessed through your presence. I will be forever grateful for your friendship."

Don Blosser
December 2014

Fred & Maggie Liechty

Author's Preface

Sometimes a door opens, and you are invited to walk through it. Once you cross the threshold, a world that has always been there suddenly becomes your world. I was once told, "You don't go looking for a best friend; you suddenly discover that you have one." Maggie Liechty was one of those friends. But we might have never met had it not been for a series of unlikely events.

In December 2007, I received a call from a seminary classmate with whom I had not been in contact in years. He asked me to consider an interim pastorate in a town about a hundred miles away. That church had not been on my radar, but Carolyn and I agreed to consider it.

In February 2008, I began a three-month interim pastorate at First Mennonite Church in Berne, Indiana. One of my first moves was to meet with church members living at Swiss Village Retirement Community. Chaplain Anita Rediger helped make the arrangements.

The pastoral assignment ended in May, and I returned to Goshen. Later that summer, Anita invited me to join her in visiting a woman she identified only as Maggie. A former First Mennonite Church member, Maggie was now living at Greencroft Retirement Community, only half a mile from our home. Anita simply said, "You will find her very interesting."

A few days later, we visited with Maggie and Fred. Maggie was more than interesting; she was captivating. A slender woman in her eighties, she was full of life, articulate, engaging, spunky, and spontaneously religious. For six years, Maggie, Fred, and I met about twice monthly exploring questions of life, faith, biblical interpretation, and whatever else came up.

Maggie and I shared the pain of Fred's death and her decision to enter hospice care about two years later. I continued to visit with her, and I began writing a daily devotional diary specifically for Maggie. Included in these devotionals were about ninety stories I'd written about people who appear in the Jesus story. They were frequently unnamed, and they usually faded from the picture after their brief encounter with Jesus.

These stories were written exclusively for Maggie. Shortly before her death on August 13, 2014, Maggie urged me to share these stories with a wider audience. During one of our last visits, she reminded me of this promise and implied she would be checking on me to be certain I did it. That was just Maggie's way!

This book is the result of a journey neither of us intended to take. It is my prayer that as you read these stories, these people will come alive for you. It's my hope this book will challenge you to share your own story of hope, struggle, disappointment, and celebration so that you will meet Jesus today in the form of friends and neighbors who are part of the worldwide community of the "Followers of Jesus" who meant so much to Maggie.

Thank you for reading. I'd be honored to hear your story at donwb@goshen.edu.

There are two things that satisfy the soul: people and stories.
And the stories have to be about people!
—G. K. Chesterton

Storytelling: A Window into Understanding

We all have stories. Behind every story is a life experience that shaped who we are and what we do. Often, we need someone else to help us tell our stories.

The Bible is filled with stories about people and their experiences in daily living interrupted by something unusual—an encounter with Jesus. In most of these stories, we are told almost nothing about the person involved. Often, they are not even named, only identified as "a Canaanite woman," or "a blind man," "a leper," and so on. We slide past them because we're trying to learn something about Jesus because we believe that's why the story is being told.

When we ignore these unnamed persons or push them to the side, we treat them exactly as they had been treated in their culture. We assume they were unimportant props helping tell the story of Jesus. Jesus, however, took a different approach; he gave them value as he focused his attention on them. He saw them as important, quite in contrast with his culture, in which they had no voice, no advocate, and often no identity.

It is important to recognize the role of storytelling in the ancient world. Our modern world expects truth to be communicated in a historically accurate detailing of events. If things didn't take place exactly as a story described them, we question whether the story itself is true. But in the ancient world, storytelling was the widely accepted way of truth telling. Tribal or family truths were communicated by wrapping them in a story. These stories were also told, maybe created, as a way to convey important religious beliefs. The message in the story was far more important than the facts and details in the story itself. This is still true in some cultures. Marcus Borg tells of the American Indian storyteller: "Now I don't know if it happened exactly this way or not, but I know this story is true."*

Jesus was an engaging storyteller, and many stories were told about him. Some stories Jesus told were parables, valuable teaching tools. We are not troubled by whether there really was a woman who diligently searched her house for a lost coin or whether an actual farmer was sowing seeds. The

---

* Seminar presentation, Trinity Cathedral, Portland, Oregon, June 2008.

message in the parable is not dependent on the actual existence of the woman or the farmer sowing his seed.

For most people, the stories Jesus told were not a problem. It is when we get into the stories told about Jesus that we have different expectations regarding truth. Jesus was a charismatic figure, and the faith community told stories to help its members remember what they believed about Jesus and what he had taught them. They shared these concepts by telling stories about Jesus. Some stories were based on actual events in Jesus' life. These were usually very personal stories for which no one was taking notes on exactly what Jesus said nor whether he actually did what the stories report.

The New Testament writers were storytellers, not historians as we use that term today. For at least thirty or more years, the faith community told these stories without having written accounts to verify the technical accuracy of what was said or what had happened.

It's quite possible that most of the stories had a specific event or encounter that did happen. It's also possible some stories were created without a factual, historical basis but to communicate a composite of truth about who Jesus was and what he did. These stories tell us much more about what the early faith community believed *about* Jesus than they do about the precise things Jesus *did*.

These gospel accounts frequently presented Jesus as a miracle worker, a healer, one who forgave sins. They often focused on how Jesus related to people whom the religious community tended to reject as sinners or the unclean. Most scholars accept the reputation of Jesus as a friend of sinners. Some stories were created to support and expand that reputation.

Many other stories about Jesus circulated during the first century. The gospels of Matthew, Mark, and Luke were not the only accounts of the life and message of Jesus the early faith community knew. There were other "gospel" accounts—the gospels of Peter, Mary, Thomas, James, and others—none of which had been written by the person named in the title. These gospels were rejected by the early church because that early faith community believed they didn't have the ring of truth in how they remembered Jesus. They included some stories found in the Matthew, Mark, and Luke accounts, but they also included other stories that glorified the person and actions of Jesus in quite bizarre, wildly exaggerated ways.

We recognize these stories as being unrealistic because we have the Matthew, Mark, and Luke stories for comparison. But the early Christians didn't have any "authoritative" documents. The gospel of Luke, written more than forty years after Jesus' death, opens with a reference to these stories (cf. Luke 1:1–4), and Luke indicates his intention to provide more-believable information. We are confident that Luke never met Jesus. He relied on the oral tradition of storytelling and on Mark's written account for his information.

Thus it's quite valid to ask, "Is this story true?" Scholars are not of one mind on how to answer that question. Some Jesus-following scholars will argue the message certainly has the ring of truth to it, but they question whether Jesus actually performed the deed described in a given story. For them, the important focus is on the message of the story, not its technical details.

Other scholars do not share this approach to the life and deeds of Jesus. This second group insists we must accept each story exactly as the biblical storyteller told it, especially the miraculous conclusion given in many of these event-stories. These discussions usually revolve around whether we should focus on the message of the story or on the details of how it is told.

These differences usually plunge the Christian community into intense arguments over Scripture, how Scripture was written, and how it should be read and interpreted. In many settings, that would be a very legitimate discussion to have. This book chooses to address the biblical stories without engaging the historical/critical question or the process vs. content debate. This book neither validates nor challenges the historic truth of the stories.

The gospel writers told these stories for a specific purpose—to strengthen readers' understanding of and commitment to the person and teachings of Jesus. With that goal in mind, I do not attempt to resolve the issue regarding the divine/human nature of Jesus or the miracle or psychological explanation of any event. My intention is to provide cultural background, social experience, and human interaction with Jesus so readers can understand the emotional dimensions of life for the person or the group identified in any one story.

These persons came to Jesus with lives filled with drama, tension, despair, and hope. Each person was on a journey that shaped who he or she was and what his or her needs were. These life stories have to be created because the gospel writers give very little information about the person. At the same time, we do know how lepers were treated, the social difficulties facing those who were blind, and the limitations placed on women. I have attempted to create realistic portrayals of these person's lives all the while recognizing these are literary, artistic creations, not historical data.

I hope this will entice the reader to read the biblical stories involved with new insight into these person's experiences to gain a better understanding of the social impact the culture had upon them. If the reader is led to say, "I never thought it about it that way!" this adventure in storytelling will be a resounding success.

I don't know if there was a blind man healed by washing in the pool of Siloam. However, we do know many blind people in Jerusalem lived without any hope of ever seeing again. I don't know if there was a Canaanite woman who brought her daughter to Jesus, but we do know the tensions present in Canaanite/Jewish marriages. The woman's encounter with Jesus at Jacob's well reveals several levels of the distrust between Jew and Samaritan. While we cannot reconstruct the exact conversation that took place that afternoon, the content reflects the reality that this woman lived with every day. This is how the story was shared in the faith community. The woman caught in the act of adultery is usually seen as a sinful woman, but when we notice the absence of any man and the accepting, nonjudgmental attitude of Jesus plus the vulnerable plight of young widows in that culture, we realize perhaps her situation could be seen differently.

We are all people who live in particular settings and under conditions unique to us. Still today, we understand others better when we walk with them in their life situations. When these individual persons met Jesus, in most cases, their lives were changed for the better. If we could sense more accurately how life was for these persons, we might be better able to accept and live with our realties.

When we do that, those first-century persons might just open the door for healing and hope in our lives. By hearing their stories, we might more easily hear and understand the stories of people around us who also need mercy, forgiveness, healing, and acceptance.

The message of Jesus is still a valid God message. We need to hear their stories so we can have the courage to tell our own stories about how that message has shaped our lives. I hope this book will help each of us become better storytellers.

1. I Wasn't Expecting This!

As a young girl, I remember my parents taking me to the synagogue where the rabbis told us stories from our Scriptures about how God spoke to our ancestors via messengers or angels. Those were always such nice stories. An angel comes and delivers a message and wonderful things happen. Being contacted by God for a specific purpose was always interpreted as a marvelous tribute to one's spirituality, for God contacts only those who are worthy of such messages.

I never thought of myself as especially worthy of anything, and I was certainly not expecting an angelic visitor. Such visits were for men, men of special distinction. I was only a girl with not much going for her. Let me tell you how it was.

I was born into a pretty typical family in Nazareth. Already, that tells you we were among the poor of the land, because Nazareth was noted for its poverty. People didn't choose to come here to live or raise families. But it was home for those of us who lived here, and we made it the best home we could. My parents were good, loving, caring people. Father was a farmer who worked the land for its owner, who lived in Jerusalem. We made a living, but life was hard. It revolved around our religious faith, our friends, and our little town, where everyone knew everyone.

I was about sixteen when my parents told me that the parents of a young man, Joseph, had come to see them, asking whether they would agree to a marriage between me and their son. I knew Joseph. He was a good man, about ten years older than I was, but that was often the way it was in our village. I was surprised but delighted because that guaranteed me security and stability—a good future.

As Joseph and I began to learn about each other I liked the way he treated me. He was a very kind man, and he really wanted to make me happy. We shared a common religious faith. That was important for me although neither of us had had any religious training. He was a carpenter, and I trusted he would provide for us. The further we got in our year of engagement, the more I was convinced I was a very fortunate woman with a good future.

Nobody told me how it would be to have an angel show up in my world. I was alone in the garden not far from our house. I was badly frightened because out of nowhere, this man I didn't recognize appeared and started talking to me. That was not how we did things in Nazareth. I guess he saw how frightened I was because he told me not to be afraid; he just needed to tell me something.

He told me I would become pregnant and have a son. My first thought was, *You know I'm not married yet.* This angel said he knew that. He said the Holy Spirit would make this happen, and my son would be a great person God would use in wonderful ways. He told me my aunt Elizabeth was expecting. I wondered how he knew that because none of our family had heard anything about it. I was surprised but very pleased because Elizabeth was quite old, and I knew she wanted a child.

I was still trying to make sense of this, but I told the messenger I trusted God and would do whatever God wanted me to do. All of a sudden, just as he came, he was gone. I went home and told my parents about the visitor and what he had told me about Joseph and me having a son. That would have been good news for any young woman planning to be married soon, but I decided not to say anything to Joseph just then. That was a bit too personal to share with him before we got married. The message from the visitor made me so happy and gave me so much to look forward to.

You can imagine my astonishment when the next month, I missed my regular menstrual period. That bothered me, but I knew it could happen, so I didn't make a fuss about it. But when it happened the second month, I knew something was wrong. I told my mother about it, and she was very upset. She wanted to know what Joseph and I had been doing. Didn't we know we weren't supposed to do that before we were married? I pleaded with her to believe me; I said we had not done anything. But she was angry.

"Young woman, I know how these things happen. How could you do this to us? You'll tell your father when he gets in from the field."

It was even harder to tell my father. He didn't get angry with me. Instead, he was furious with Joseph for doing this to me. I told him again and again that it hadn't been Joseph, that we hadn't done anything. But he didn't believe me. He and Mother went off by themselves to talk about me and decide how they would handle this situation.

While they were talking to each other, I decided I would just have to tell them again about what the angel said, how the Holy Spirit was going to make this happen, and how they had to trust I was telling the truth. Do you know what it's like to be fifteen, to never have had sex with anyone, and yet be pregnant and not have your mother and father believe you? If I had known this was what the angel meant when he said I would become pregnant, I might have thought a bit longer before agreeing. Is this what happens when you follow God? That was not how the rabbis told the stories.

Mother and Father came back with a decision. I had to tell Joseph and beg his forgiveness for what I had done. They didn't want to believe it, but the evidence was there, and they said I'd have to deal with it,

I lay down that night, but I didn't sleep. What was God trying to tell me? How had this happened? The angel had made it sound like such a good thing. Why was it turning out so awfully? Why didn't my parents believe me? What would Joseph do? What was I going to do?

The next evening, I met with Joseph. I had thought very carefully about how I was going to tell him. I told him in detail about the angel coming, what the angel had said, and how I had agreed to accept what God was asking me to do.

I don't know what I was expecting from Joseph, but he didn't believe me either. He looked at me for a few moments without saying a word. Finally, he spoke. "Mary, how could you do this to me? I trusted you. Who was it? Tell me the truth. Don't give me this story about an angel messenger from God. I don't believe you."

I nearly collapsed. I fought back tears. I wanted to scream. I tried to speak, but no sounds came out of mouth. That was when I knew my life was over. All the dreams I'd had about marriage and the joy of raising a child were gone. I knew I hadn't done anything wrong, but no one believed me. When I looked up, I saw Joseph walking away from me. I was all alone. I wanted to die.

I went home and told my parents. They tried to be understanding, but they were also devastated. The next day, a message came from Joseph's parents, informing my parents that our marriage was off and that Joseph wanted no more contact with me. I sat down in a dark corner of our little house and cried and cried and cried. It wasn't fair! I was doing only what God had asked me to do, so why was my world falling apart? What hope was there for a young woman like me? What was going to happen to me?

Mary's story is told in Luke 1:36–3:20.

2. Why Is This So Hard?

I was wondering what I was going to do when a message came from Jerusalem telling us about Elizabeth and Zechariah's good news. Elizabeth was six months pregnant, and they were so happy. I suggested to Mother that perhaps I could go to Jerusalem and be of some help to Aunt Elizabeth in the final months of her pregnancy because of her age. It would give me an excuse to get out of Nazareth for a while. The arrangements were quickly made and two days later I left for Jerusalem.

Elizabeth was so glad to see me. I told her about the angel and that I was pregnant. I was so relieved that she wasn't shocked. She actually believed me and told me how it was with her and Zechariah. I knew right away that Aunt Elizabeth and I would get along perfectly well. I felt that my time with her might help heal the pain I was living with. I never gave up hope that Joseph might contact me. I knew it would never happen, but the hope gave me the courage to get up each morning. Maybe today!

Why is it that when you hope and hope and pray and pray for something, when it actually does happen, you still can't believe it? I will never forget that day. It was early afternoon nearly two months later when my father showed up at Zechariah and Elizabeth's door with a message from Joseph. He had actually said that he was sorry for the way he had treated me. He said that he had had a dream, or a visit by an angel—he wasn't sure which—but he wanted me to come home so we could pick up our plans to get married. He told me he would be a father for my child and we would make it work. Would I please come home?

My first response was, "I can't go now. Elizabeth is expecting to deliver any day. I have to stay with her." But Elizabeth was very firm. "Yes, you can go, and you will go. Right now!" So the next day, I returned to Nazareth to face Joseph. I was ecstatic and scared at the same time. Dare I believe this is really happening?

Joseph came that evening and told me about what it had been like when I was gone. How he had been awake at night and had prayed and struggled trying to figure out what the right thing to do was. In the process, he said, "I started thinking. What if you had been telling the truth. We had made plans," he said. He wanted us to make those plans work. And then, right in front of my parents, he reached for my hand, gave it a squeeze, and didn't let go. I was so wonderfully happy that I didn't remember he wasn't supposed to hold my hand yet!

My parents were so thankful. It took Joseph's parents a little longer to accept this, but they gradually did, and we made plans to be married in a few months. But that month, Joseph got the notice that we had to go to Bethlehem to register for a Roman census. We tried to reason with the local Roman officials, but they would not listen. We had a three-month period during which we had to register, so we decided to do it as soon as we could. That way, we could register and be back in Nazareth before the baby was due. My parents and I began making plans for the wedding.

That trip to Bethlehem was much worse than I had expected. We took one of the farm donkeys and a two-wheeled cart for me to ride in. It took three days, and the roads were hard, but we got there. We weren't sure what to expect, so we got in line right away. That was probably a mistake. We should have found a room for the night first.

We were standing in line when a young Roman soldier came over and asked us to come with him. Joseph wasn't sure we should give up our place in line; you never could trust Roman soldiers. But he seemed to be a nice young man, so we went with him. He helped us register, and in just a short time, we were done.

Then we began our search for a room. Joseph tried hard, but his patience was wearing thin after the third place. And I was beginning to have labor pains. They weren't supposed to come for another three weeks, when we would be back in Nazareth. But they were coming, and I was frightened. We were a long way from home, and I was alone. This was not what we had planned.

At one place, the innkeeper's wife said we could use their barn. She saw I was in labor and needed help. She told me the barn was clean, the night was warm, and she would help me with the baby.

So we ended up in a stable. That woman was so helpful; I don't know what I would have done without her. She brought blankets and food and stayed with me until the baby had come. What a night! I was exhausted, but all had gone well, given the circumstances.

As I lay there with the baby asleep in my arms, I reflected on what I had been through. In the space of one year, I had begun plans to get married, I had seen an angel, I had become pregnant, I had been rejected by my husband-to-be, and all my plans for marriage had been cancelled. Then I had several months with Aunt Elizabeth, Joseph had changed his mind and wanted us to get married, and we were in Bethlehem, where I'd just given birth in a stable to a healthy baby boy. What else did God have in mind for me? I remember hoping that now perhaps, life would become more normal for all of us.

Oh yes. I almost forgot to tell you about the shepherds. I had awakened in the middle of the night and was just looking in admiration at my baby when the innkeeper's wife told us there were three shepherds who wanted to see the baby. *Three shepherds? What's going on here?* I wondered. But she said she would stay to be sure it was okay, so I agreed and they came in.

Their story was really interesting but sort of unbelievable. They had seen an angel—another angel?—who told them to go see my baby. One shepherd said a very nice brief prayer for us, and then they left. Once again, I lay there with the baby, trying to figure out what all this meant.

The next morning, we were able to move into a room in the inn. Joseph actually found temporary work as a carpenter, and the innkeeper helped us find a small but adequate one-room house where we could stay until I was strong enough to go home.

But two weeks later, we had another surprise. This one was even more unusual. Three royalty persons from a foreign country that I had never heard of were at our door. They told of having seen a combination of stars and a constellation in the sky that had led them to us.

I didn't know what they were talking about. We Jewish people don't believe in astrological messages from the stars. But they were very kind, and they stayed only a short time. The most astounding thing was what they gave us. I had never seen gold before, and they gave us some gold coins—actually, a lot of gold coins—and some other very nice gifts. They told me my baby was a very special child. I remembered that was exactly what the angel had told me back in Nazareth.

We shared stories, and after a few hours, they left. But the next morning, one of them was back. In frantic tones, he told us we had to get out of the country right away. He was afraid King Herod would do something awful to us if he found us. I asked why anyone would want to hurt a baby. He said he wasn't sure, but he just felt something bad was going to happen and we had to leave right away. He told us there was a caravan going to Egypt, leaving that morning, and we had to go with it. He even gave us more money to pay for it. He told us to take the money and he would sell our donkey and cart, but we had to leave!

We joined the caravan, and by midmorning, we were on our way south toward Egypt. I wondered, *Is this the way life is going to be for us?* Were we running away from something without even knowing what it was? Would we ever return to Nazareth?

—Mary's story is told in Matthew 1:18–2:15 and Luke 1:26–2:20.

3. How Could She Do This to Me?

Nazareth is a pleasant little town nestled in the foothills of Galilee about four miles from the Roman supply city of Sepphoris and sixty-five miles north of Jerusalem. Living in the shadow of Sepphoris meant the constant presence of the Roman military because that was their central base in Galilee. But I was in training to be a carpenter, and the Nazareth economy benefited from the Roman presence.

With the assurance of work, I asked my parents to meet with the parents of a young girl named Mary. I wanted to ask their permission to marry her when she was older. I had very little to offer except the promise to be a good husband. Both our families were poor, and we knew what life would be like as a new family. But I was a good worker, a trusted person, and I knew I could provide for Mary responsibly. We had known each other for years, having grown up together in Nazareth. She was younger than me, but that was not unusual in Nazareth.

We were delighted when they agreed, but as yet, nothing had been said to anyone else. We agreed that when she would turn seventeen, we would plan for our wedding. This was a very satisfying decision, and I was glad to see my future had promise. I was indeed fortunate.

That's how we did it. On her seventeenth birthday, the announcement was made, and we began the year of wedding preparation. The cultural rules for that year were very strict and well known. We were not to be alone in any private way. We had virtually no physical contact of any kind, although I did hold her hand a few times and was rewarded with the warmest smile I'd ever seen.

About halfway through the year, I sensed something was not going well. Mary was withdrawing and becoming quiet. She seemed troubled about something, but I could not get her to talk about it. That is, until "that" day, one I will never forget. I can still walk you through almost every moment of it.

Mary came to me that afternoon and said, "We have to talk." What she had to talk about was horrible! Devastating in more ways than I could imagine. It started out okay. She told me she cared about me more than anything else. She told me about a visit she had had from an angel. That surprised me, because I knew there were stories about such things in our Jewish history, but that hadn't happened for several hundred years. But I kept listening until she grabbed my hand, held it tightly, and said, "Joseph, I'm pregnant."

I yanked my hand away and took two steps back. "You're *what?*" She started to cry and tried to offer the most unbelievable explanation. "Joseph, I have not been with any man. I have been faithful to you, and I want to be your wife, just like we planned. The angel told me this would happen and that it would be by God's Holy Spirit, not by any man. Joseph, you have to believe me. I have not done anything wrong. The child I'm carrying is God's child. I have not had sex with anyone."

I had never heard anything so ridiculous. What unbelievable lies! Did she really expect me to believe *God* had made her pregnant? That would be a first!

I didn't know what to say so I turned and walked away. How could she have done this to me? How could she have lied about it? In those few minutes, my future crumbled. I would be the object of ridicule and gossip. What did she think I would do?

For three days, I stayed away from work, claiming I was sick. I didn't talk to anyone. I couldn't sleep; I didn't want to eat. I couldn't go on that way. She had ruined our relationship in a way that could never be restored. I spent a lot of time thinking about my options. I could still marry her, but people would be quick to do the math. When the baby was born, they would blame me, and my reputation would be gone. I knew it hadn't been me, and for the rest of my life I would be raising some other man's child if I went through with the marriage. I knew I would never be able to forget that.

I could denounce her publicly, identifying her for what she really was, and it was likely she would be stoned for violating her commitment to me. I knew I couldn't marry her given what she had done to me. I also knew I couldn't find it in myself to pronounce a death sentence on her by publicly condemning her. After all, I had planned on marrying her!

I wrestled with these ideas until the pain was so great I couldn't bear it. I decided on the only option I could live with. I sent word to her that the relationship was over, that we would not get married, that she was on her own, and that I never wanted to see her again.

I didn't know what she would do. I didn't even know what I was going to do. Have you ever felt that your life had ended even though you wake up every morning and have to face another day?

About a week later, a friend told me Mary had left town. He was wondering why? What was going on with us. I told him I didn't want to talk about it. He accepted that, but I knew it didn't satisfy him. I later found out Mary had gone to visit her aunt Elizabeth in Jerusalem. I was glad. That meant I wouldn't see her on the street. That would have been embarrassing.

The next two, three months were awful. I went to work, but my heart wasn't in it. I could hardly eat or sleep. One night, I was lying awake on my bed thinking. Mary and I had had a good life planned for us. We were a good fit. Everybody makes a mistake once in a while, and we have to learn to live with that. Even I had done some things I wish I hadn't, but certainly nothing as bad as what she had done to me. How could she have done that? What had she been thinking? That made me wonder. She wouldn't have voluntarily done anything like that. That was not who she was. What if some Roman soldier had taken advantage of her? They did that, you know. And if she had tried to fight him off, and she certainly would have tried, but any Roman soldier would have overpowered her. What if it wasn't her fault?

I remembered a verse in the Torah that said if a woman is raped and she tried to stop it, she should not be judged because she had done nothing wrong. What if that had happened to Mary? I began to sob uncontrollably as I imagined what she must have been through and how I had added to her pain by rejecting her. My crying soon sapped my strength and I fell asleep. During the night I dreamed that an angel came, telling me I should trust Mary because she had done nothing wrong; she really was telling the truth.

I woke up with a start. I tried to sort out what this meant. Was I dreaming, or did that angel really happen? I had to talk with Mary. There was no reason to let one mistake ruin her life, and mine too—especially when it wasn't her fault. We had a good life planned. If we would get married, we could raise the child together. I could love it as if it were my own. I would have to adjust to this new life, but I could do that. I thought about it for a day. I decided to see if Mary and I could work things out.

The next day, I wrote a message to Elizabeth, asking her to talk to Mary for me because I wasn't sure if Mary would want to hear what I had to say. After all, I hadn't listened to what she had had to say. I asked Elizabeth to tell Mary I'd thought about it for a long time and I was asking her to come home. Let's get married just as we'd planned. I promised we would raise the child as though it were mine. We had had good dreams for the future. Let's get married and start rebuilding our lives together. Will you come home?

That afternoon, I went to her parents' home and talked with them about what I was asking of Mary. I asked her father if he would deliver my message to Elizabeth. They were so relieved. They knew Mary would never have done anything like that to me. While they had not known what to think when Mary told them about the angel, they had understood what I felt I had to do. They were grateful I wasn't going to make a public spectacle of their daughter, and they promised their enthusiastic support for our marriage. Mary's father said he would go right away and urge Mary to come home.

I left their house feeling good. What if Mary was right and all this was just like she had said it was? I knew it would remain a mystery. All that angel stuff was more than I could understand, but then, there are lots of things I don't understand. I can live with that.

—Joseph's story is in Matthew 1:18–25.

4. How Can This Be?

I decided Mary and I should get married right away. Delaying things would raise only more questions. We planned for a quick and quiet wedding and began getting ready for the baby. Mary's parents were really helpful with things we needed. Mary was doing well, and we were expecting a normal final two months of her pregnancy. And then we got that notice. It came as a Roman proclamation that was posted all over town. You couldn't miss it.

All citizens were required to report to their family homes for a national census. We all knew what that meant. It didn't mention taxes, but for the past ten years, the local Roman officials had been gathering data about everyone in town. Most of us hadn't paid much attention. We weren't fighting it; we just weren't participating. But just the previous month, we had heard that Quirinius, the acting governor of Syria, had come to Palestine with the Roman military to finalize this census registration. Everybody knew about Quirinius. He was brutal on the local people and ruled Syria with a massive military force.

Quirinius decided to speed up the process by demanding everyone register in person in his parental family hometown. That was new. And there was a deadline. I talked to the local Roman military officers about Mary's condition. They told me there would be no exceptions. Mary and I had three months to make the trip to Bethlehem. We talked about it and decided it was best to go right away so we could get back to Nazareth at least three weeks before she was due. It certainly wasn't what either of us wanted, but we had no choice. Two weeks later, we left for Bethlehem.

It was not a good trip. We had a small cart for Mary to ride in, but the roads were bumpy and the trip was long. I could tell it was taking a toll on her. The Roman military could be so stubborn. I didn't understand why I couldn't have gone by myself. But the penalty for not having Mary with me was severe, so you do what the army says.

I walked, muttering under my breath, while the donkey pulled the cart. I had a lot on my mind. How were we going to pay for this trip on top of the preparations for the baby? It just seemed the world was trying to be unfair. Wealthy people went past us in their enclosed carriages pulled by two-horse teams. Not one of them showed any interest in helping us, and no one offered to let Mary ride with them. I guess I was showing my frustration because Mary said, "Joseph, please don't be upset. God has promised to take care of us. We'll be okay." We kept plodding toward Bethlehem.

We arrived in mid-afternoon of the third day. I asked Mary if she could handle doing the registration first and finding a room after that. She agreed, so we got in line. One Roman soldier who was supervising the process saw Mary, came over, and told us to come with him. I wasn't comfortable doing that, but Mary thought we should. He took us to a table and asked us four or five questions, and we were finished. Back home, Roman soldiers often made you line up and stand there for no reason at all, but this soldier had even asked Mary how she was feeling, how far we had come, and when she was due. Maybe he had a wife and family back home. Maybe God hadn't forgotten about us.

I turned to Mary. "Good. That's done. Now let's find a room so you can get some rest. I saw an inn back there on the way in. It didn't look too expensive. Let's go there."

At the inn, I helped Mary out of the cart and we went up to the door. "We'd like a room for the night, please," I said to the man at the door.

"Oooh, sorry sir, we don't have anything available. You might try down the street." He pointed to a small building not far away. "They have more room than I do."

Mary climbed back into the cart, and we went down the street. I breathed a short prayer to Yahweh as we went up to the door and asked the same question. "Sorry, we're full," the innkeeper said. "Could you suggest a place?" I asked.

"Why yes. Just go up the street on the other side. He's my friend. Good place."

"We've already been there. He sent us here."

"Oh. Well, let's see. There's another place on the other side of town, maybe twenty minutes from here. It's a little out of the way, so they'll probably have room."

So we went there. That time, Mary stayed in the cart. I was glad she did because the owner swore at me and told us, "Get out of here! Lot of nerve you have trying to get a room at this hour."

Trying not to show my frustration, I told Mary, "They don't have any room either." I was really angry with myself. I started apologizing to Mary, telling her this is no way to treat a wife and how awful I felt about what she was going through.

But Mary calmly said, "Joseph, you're doing the best you can. It isn't your fault. I appreciate what you are doing. We'll get a room. I know we will. Only we better hurry."

I looked at her and realized what she meant as her eyes went shut, and her whole body became tense for a moment. I knew I had to find a room at any price. But at every stop, the answer was the same, and every time, the door was shut in my face. I got more frustrated and more angry. *How could this be?*

We quickly ran out of options. In desperation, we went back to the first inn. I hoped beyond hope that maybe they could help. But the answer was still the same. "We can't help. We have nothing, I am truly sorry."

With that, I got frantic. "You don't understand! My wife is having a baby. You have to help us." I guess my voice got a little loud, because the man's wife came to the door to see what was happening. She saw Mary in the cart and immediately went to talk with her. I tried to argue with the innkeeper but was getting nowhere when his wife said something to him that made me even more angry. I heard her say something about how they might have some space in the barn. That was more than I could take. "The *barn?* You think I would take my wife to a barn?" But just then I heard Mary say, "Joseph, take it. We'd better take it, right now!"

I had never felt more like a failure. We went behind the inn to the barn. I felt miserable. I wanted to cry out in anger, shake my fist at God, do something, anything to express what I was feeling. *How can this be? A barn! What is God trying to do to us?*

But when I saw the barn, I calmed down just a bit. It wasn't that bad. The innkeeper's wife told us their children had often slept out there with their friends. It was warm and dry, and we could be off by ourselves. It was certainly a lot better than being out on the street with drunken Roman soldiers.

The innkeeper's wife was very nice. She brought hot soup and bread, a lantern, and some extra blankets. But when I saw Mary putting straw in the feed trough and folding a blanket to cover it, I went off in the corner and kicked the stable wall. Hard! *This isn't fair! How can this be?*

The innkeeper's wife stayed to help Mary with her delivery. It was only a few hours later when Mary called me over, "Joseph, come, it's a boy, aren't you proud?"

I was proud. Of Mary, of the baby, of everybody but me. Our first child is born in a stable. *What must Mary think of me?* But when I sat down beside Mary, as she was propped up on a clean blanket, she showed me the baby, and suddenly it wasn't so bad. The baby was here, healthy, and Mary ... I was so proud of her. She had done so well.

Soon after that, Mary fell asleep with the baby sleeping in her arms. I heard a creak at the barn door, and in came some shepherds who had the strangest story about some angels who told them to come see this baby. It was okay, but I couldn't imagine why angels would do that. Why us? Their excited whispering woke Mary, and she carefully lifted the corner of the blanket so they could see the baby.

Mary smiled as one of the older shepherds with tears streaming down his cheeks knelt beside her, kissed her on the forehead, and prayed, "Lord God, Father of Abraham, Isaac and Jacob, we thank you for this night, and we pray you would watch over this child ..." His voice trailed off as if he didn't know what else to say. But I was touched by it. I wondered, *How can this be?*

—This Joseph story is in Matthew 1:18–25.

5. A Roman Soldier

I am Cornelius. I was on my first tour of duty in the Roman army and was fortunate to have received deployment in Palestine. Rome was solidly in control of the area and the country was peaceful; our task was to keep it that way. The order from Rome to take over the census was not unusual. We were there, we were trained to do administrative work, and we were not actively fighting any war, so it gave us something to do. We knew the general population didnot like it because while it was publicized as a census, everyone knew that gathering information was the first step in raising taxes.

But these people should have recognized what we were doing for them. We were keeping the country safe for travel, we built roads, we were constructing badly needed government buildings, plus the army bought food and other supplies from local businesses. As I see it, we are the good guys. They have no reason to hate us for doing our job. I can only imagine what this country would be like if we were not here. They should be grateful. I know once in a while we have to arrest someone, try them, and even execute those who are a threat to Rome. We have a saying: "It is better to kill one man than to have him cause trouble that leads to the death of a dozen people."

I planned to make a career of service in the military. The pay isn't good for the average soldier, but I know that if I stayed with it and moved up the ranks, I'll do okay. It is a good job. I have been in Palestine for about six months. In another six months I will return home for one month with my parents. I am going to get married, and after my first promotion in two years, my wife will be permitted to join me here.

Conducting the census is really boring work. There are forms to fill out, statistics to be kept, and reports to be made every month. That is one thing we Romans know how to do. We are good at keeping records. This is simple. You set up a table, people come to you. We need to have their name, where they live, the names of their wife and children with their ages, occupations, and what property they own. Everyone had to come in person. We cannot accept having them tell us they have a wife and three children back home. We have to count and validate everyone. On some days the line can be pretty long. People don't like that, but that is just how it is.

Late one afternoon, we were really busy when I saw this young couple join the line. My task that day was to keep the line moving and make sure nobody caused any problems for the soldiers taking the information. That's when I saw she was pregnant. Really pregnant. And she looked exhausted. Most of the time, that wouldn't matter. We have a job to do, and the people can stand in line or come back the next day. That's their choice. But I estimated they would be in line for about two hours before reaching the census table. It just didn't seem right to make her do that in her condition, so I picked up a registration form and told them to come with me. We found an empty table, and I gave her a bench to sit down. She appreciated that, I could tell. I asked them the questions and completed the whole registration process in about fifteen minutes. I found they had been married about two months and were expecting their first child in about two weeks. Yes, I could do the math, but I didn't say anything because that was their business.

I told them I was going to be married in a couple of months and hoped we would have children too. I wished them well, and they went on their way. I went back to work and forgot about them.

That is, until about three hours later, after we had closed down for the day. I was on my way back to camp when I saw them making their way slowly down one of the narrow, dirty side streets. I wondered why they hadn't found a place to stay. I didn't say anything. It wasn't my problem. But I thought to myself, goodness, I hope they find a place soon. It was getting dark, and they should have been off the streets by now.

Skip Ahead about Thirty Years ...

I'm married now, have two children, and have risen in the ranks to centurion. Most of my career has been in Jerusalem. Two years ago, I received a command appointment in Caesarea, a much better post than Jerusalem. Things have become quite tense in Jerusalem. A Jewish sect, the Zealots, have become much more active. We call them terrorists. They are a dangerous group. If they catch a Roman soldier alone, they will attack him. We've lost several soldiers that way. We wear uniforms so people know who we are. But zealots don't wear uniforms; they could be anybody, so we have given strict orders that no soldier leave camp alone. We have to travel in twos or threes for our safety.

I heard just a couple of months ago that things really exploded in Jerusalem. Herod Antipas is a hothead. They had captured two zealots who were scheduled for execution. Somehow, a Jewish religious prophet got caught up in all that. The religious leaders did not like him; exactly why I don't know. Herod got pulled into it. He gave in to Jewish pressure, and three people were crucified. I'm not sure I would have handled it that way if I had been in charge. I think there has to be other, better options. You don't always keep the peace by killing people.

Skip Ahead Five More Years ...

I am now about ready to retire. My wife and I have decided to stay here in Caesarea. It's a nice city, more peaceful than most, and she has made lots of friends. Our children are grown and have their own families. This feels like home. We have learned the language, understand the culture, and actually have a good number of Jewish friends. They aren't bad people; they just have strong religious values. But they do a really good job of taking care of each other. I have learned to appreciate that. I have also learned that my theories about how to keep the peace actually work. I have tried to use my influence in using the military to work at community projects. We use local workers whenever possible, and I have insisted that my soldiers have special training in Jewish culture so we don't create unnecessary problems.

We did something two years ago that I am proud of. My wife had made friends with some Jewish women, and she had even begun attending synagogue rather regularly. I was impressed with what she was learning and how they let her help with some good projects.

I even went with her once in a while to synagogue. I knew about the Roman pantheon of gods but never paid much attention to them. She was intrigued with the concept that there was only one God. That made sense to me. It certainly made religion a lot simpler. I didn't join the synagogue—Roman soldiers didn't do that—but I supported my wife in several of the religious things she did. I even joined with her in prayers and in helping the poor in Caesarea. I guess I had caught the vision of these people about the positive benefits of helping other people.

She was the one who told me about the synagogue in Caesarea that had been destroyed some ten years ago by the regional government. I checked into it, and she was right. Once again, it was Herod thinking he could control people by making life more difficult for them. He didn't understand how these people think and how important their religious faith is for them. So I filed a petition with Rome. We got the authorization and the financial support to build a new "community center." Technically, it's a synagogue, but they do other community projects at the synagogue too. I should tell Herod that he could keep the peace by working with people, not by fighting them and destroying their religious institutions.

It was about then that I first met some Jewish people who were talking about a prophet teacher named Jesus. They talked about a new way of doing things, of helping the poor, about worship, about telling the truth, about respect for women and children, and about loving your enemies. Most of it made sense except for that "loving your enemies" foolishness. I knew from personal experience that doesn't work.

One day, my wife asked me if we could invite one of their leaders to our house to see what this group was all about. I wanted to know whether they were going to be a threat to Rome and what their specific goals were, so I agreed.

A man named Peter came and spent a day with us. He explained who they were and what their goals were. I had some questions about this teacher Jesus and what he had done that Rome had crucified him. I remembered hearing about that. I knew that sometimes Rome had crucified innocent people by mistake—those things happen—but I needed to know the truth. Peter explained it, and when he told me Herod was involved, it made sense.

It all made sense. Most of what Peter said was about values my wife and I already had. These were things we were already doing with our lives. We told Peter he could count on us for support for what they were doing. We didn't officially join anything because I was still a Roman soldier, but we quietly became active in the group. I wasn't sure what this would mean for my military career, but I was close to retirement. If anyone in Rome made a fuss, I would just retire.

One thing I've wondered about. Peter told us Jesus had been born in Bethlehem just a couple of months before Herod the Great had died. I tried to figure backward. I'd been in Bethlehem that year, helping with the Roman census on my first tour of duty. The dates fit. Could I have met the parents of Jesus? Could they have been the couple I had helped register? It's a long shot, but I sort of hoped it was them. It would be nice to think that years ago I was helping this Jesus whom I now accept as Lord.

(Remember, this story is created based on some situational data. It is extremely unlikely if not impossible that Cornelius was the same soldier who was present in Bethlehem. Perhaps the lesson for us is that we never know when we help someone, exactly who it

is we are helping. Perhaps that is a good thing, because it frees us up from making any judgments, so we can just offer help. Certainly the same presence of God that was there with Mary and Joseph was present also with Cornelius. That same presence is with us today. Who is it in our world that we should be helping?)

—The Cornelius story is in Acts 10.

6. The Innkeeper's Wife

None of us like the idea of a Roman census. We all knew it wasn't really about counting people. Rome wouldn't admit it, but it was all about raising taxes. My husband and I didn't want to benefit at the expense of others, but this census has been good for us. Bethlehem is an old town, so we had lots of people coming back to their ancestral home for the census registration. There were only a few inns in town, so we been busy. If you didn't book early in the day, you might not find a place for the night.

That's why I sighed when there was a knock at the door just as we were finished eating our evening meal. Who can that be at this hour? But I went to the door with my husband. I saw a young couple. The woman was obviously uncomfortable in her advanced pregnancy. When I patiently explained we didn't have any rooms, the man didn't take the news very well. When I suggested another place, he told me they had been there. In fact, they'd been everywhere, and we were their last hope. They had to have a room. Couldn't we do something for them?

When he raised his voice, my husband Seth tried to reason with the husband, I found myself making eye contact with the young woman. She was really young, and really pregnant. She looked frightened, and I could see tears starting to stream down her face. I remembered what it was like when Seth and I had had our first child. That was quite a few years ago, but I remembered being so frightened, and I'd had my mother and grandmother there to help.

I tried to think hard. What could we do? What did we have to offer? That's when I thought of the stable. The night was warm, so that wouldn't be a problem. Seth was so particular about keeping things clean that we used to let our children sleep out there in the summer, sort of like camping out with their friends.

I tapped Seth's shoulder. "We could let them have space in the barn, where the kids used to sleep." I tried to say it quietly, sort of under my breath so this young couple wouldn't be insulted. But the man—he told us his name was Joseph—had good ears, and he exploded in anger. "My wife is going to have a baby and you want to put us in the *barn*? What kind of people are you?"

I knew right away this could erupt into problem, and with Roman soldiers on patrol, that wouldn't be good for any of us. I left Seth to try to calm Joseph down, and I went around him to get closer to his wife. I explained to her how our children used to sleep out there for fun, how the space was private, and that it was a lot cleaner and safer than pitching a tent on the edge of town. I told her I knew what it was like, I'd had three children of my own. "We'll let you have it free. It's the best space you're going to find in town tonight." I gently squeezed her hand. "It will be okay. Trust me. It will work for one night. We'll have a room for you tomorrow evening. This is just for one night."

As I was speaking, I saw her whole body go tense with a labor pain, so I just held her tight for a moment till it passed. "Tell your husband you don't have much time."

I heard her tired, frightened voice: "Joseph, we'd better take it. Now!"

Seth and I took them around the house, back to the barn. It was still light enough to see. I was glad that we had just cleaned it. I don't know why we did, but we had a little extra time this afternoon. We tied their donkey in an empty stall and began making things as good as we could. Seth brought a thick layer of clean straw and put it in a feeding trough while I went inside to get some blankets to cover it.

I could see right away that Joseph certainly meant well, but he was not going to be much help. I knew we had some leftover soup and a little bread, so I sent Seth in to get it while Mary and I started getting things ready for the baby. Mary wasn't hungry, but it gave Joseph something to do while we women got organized.

I was impressed with Mary. She was young, but she was strong, and she knew what to do. She told me that just a few months ago she had helped her aunt Elizabeth get ready for the baby, so she thought she would be okay.

She did just fine. We got her as comfortable as we could, and we settled in to wait for the baby. I was glad I could be there with her. She was brave, and she worked hard. It took a little over two hours of good, hard labor, and the baby was here. He was not terribly big, but he was in good shape. And he had a healthy set of lungs.

I took over cleaning things up. Mary got situated on her improvised straw bed, and I gave Mary her baby boy. There was not much else for me to do. Mary indicated she was awfully tired but quite pleased with herself. I was proud of her too. She had done very well considering it was her first child. Joseph thanked me for my help and said he would take over. I thought, *Huh? Now he offers!* But I could see he really did want to do all he could.

Seth and I told Mary to send Joseph if she needed anything during the night, and we went back to the house. I told Seth, "I'm really glad we had space in the barn. I think we did the right thing. It looks like they'll get along okay tonight, and tomorrow, we can give them that room on the ground floor. Those folks will be leaving by midmorning."

About two hours later, I was still awake. After all, it wasn't every evening I delivered a baby in the barn. I heard a noise out back, so I got up and went out to see what was going on. I saw three shepherds heading toward the barn. I stopped them right away because they had no business there with that young family trying to get some rest.

They told me they had seen some angels who had told them to come here to see a baby. I told them to wait outside while I checked with the mother. Mary was awake. She said I should let them in, but she asked me to stay with her just in case, so of course I did. They had this strange story to tell her. I had never heard anything quite like it—angels singing, telling them to come to town to find a newborn in a stable? It was too crazy to have been made up. They didn't stay long, and since Mary was falling asleep again, I went back to bed.

I have often wondered what happened to that young family. They looked like such a normal, practical couple. They stayed with us for three days, then moved into an empty one-room house in town.

I hope everything went well for them. And I hope that baby boy grew up to do something good with his life.

I felt good about what we had done. I only wish we could have done more.

—This story is in Luke 2:6–7.

7. A Night to Remember

We certainly weren't expecting anything like this. It had been a long day, as most days are with sheep when you're close to town. There wasn't much to do. There were no wild animals around, and good grass and water were readily available. So when night came we divided up the watches and settled down to rest. Jebo, Ephraim, and Simon took the first watch. The rest of us wanted to get some sleep.

I woke with a start when all of a sudden the night sky just plain lit up. It wasn't the moon but a brilliant glowing in the clouds. I saw this figure coming toward us. I jumped up; tried to get my bearings, and figure out where it was in relation to town. It seemed to be hovering just above the horizon. That didn't make sense.

Jebo came running from the other side of the flock. We just stared, not knowing what it was or what it wanted. By instinct, I grabbed my staff and was ready to fight off this mysterious, invading presence. But strangely, the sheep weren't skittish. They didn't seem to be seeing anything. The light was really bright, but it was a different kind of light, not like the sun. It was just—just light!

Jebo and I were ready to defend the sheep when this strange apparition spoke to us. "Don't be afraid of me. I have good news for you that will be a blessing for everyone. The promised Messiah has been born tonight, just over the hill in Bethlehem. You will find him in a manger. The baby will be snugly wrapped in strips of cloth."

I wanted to ask a question, but I wouldn't have known what to ask even if I could have said anything at that point. I knew the rabbis had been praying for the Messiah to come save us for longer than I could remember, but I hadn't paid much attention to them. It didn't seem like God cared about what happened to us these days.

I was just standing there looking, when I blinked a couple of times. I saw a whole group of angelic figures, more than I could count, surrounding the one who had spoken to us. I recognized them from the stories I'd been taught from the Torah when I was a boy. They started to sing, and it was mesmerizing.

"Glory to God in the highest, and peace on earth to all people" or something like that; I was too stunned to get it all. With that, they were gone. Just blip, gone, and it was dark all around us.

I turned to Jebo. "What was that all about? Did you see that?"

"Yeah, I saw that, but I don't know what it was. What do we do now?"

"Let's get Ephraim and see what he thinks."

Ephraim was sort of our leader. When we told him what had happened, he laughed at us. He thought we'd just been seeing things. How come he hadn't seen it? Why didn't the sheep get scared?

Jebo and I insisted that we'd seen angels and heard them sing. Ephraim shook his head and muttered about what had gotten into us. We argued with him, but he wasn't sympathetic. That's when Jebo suggested "Jesse, let's check it out. We can be back in a couple of hours. Let's wake up the others and see if they want to go with us."

The others? Surely they would have heard the angels. But they had been sleeping and were a bit irritated that we woke them up with what they thought was a crazy story. All except for Jacob. He was the youngest in the group, and he said he wanted to come along. He thought it would be fun. The rest agreed to stand watch for us. After a short argument about the foolishness of what we were going to do, Jebo, Jacob, and I set off for Bethlehem.

On the way, we tried to work out a strategy. Go to a manger. But which one? I knew the town and told them there were only three options where there might be an empty manger these days. I suggested that we start with Seth's place. He had a barn right behind his inn that was usually half-empty.

We were going around the inn to the barn when Seth's wife Rachel came out. What was she doing up at this time of night? She stopped us and wanted to know what we were doing? I told her what we'd seen and heard and asked if they had anybody staying in the inn. I didn't take that angel too seriously about the baby being in a manger. I figured it would be in the inn. Rachel looked at me kind of funny. "There is a young family in the barn. The woman just had a baby." But she didn't think we should bother them just now. I explained again about the angels, so she agreed to see how things were with the mother. She came back in a moment and said we could go in.

I went in first. Jacob and Jebo followed me. Rachel put a candle on the ledge, and I saw the mother lying there propped up against the straw with a baby in her arms. She was really young, but she nodded to us, so I went over to her. I quietly whispered what we had seen and heard. She didn't act surprised. She just lifted the blanket covering the baby and I got to see him. I had two children of my own, so I knew not to touch him. I just looked, and then for the first time in years—at least that I can remember—I started to pray. "Lord God, Father of Abraham, Isaac, and Jacob, I thank you for this night and for this child. I pray that you would protect this family and keep them safe always."

I didn't know what else to say. Like I said, I hadn't prayed for a long time, so I just stopped. I leaned down and kissed the mother on the forehead. I hoped that was okay. I'd never done that before. She just smiled at me, so I guess it was. I thanked Rachel, nodded to Jebo and Jacob, and we left.

On the way back to the flock, we talked about what we had seen. Jacob wanted to know all about the angels. He was upset that we hadn't gotten him up. I was surprised he hadn't heard them. Jebo and I decided we knew what we'd seen, and that probably no one else would believe us, so we just weren't going to tell anyone. Why go asking for trouble?

But I couldn't figure it out. Why was I the only one to wake up? Why didn't Ephraim see or hear anything? Why had it been just Jebo and me? Had we really seen angels? That doesn't happen very often. Why us? There were lots of people more important than us, so why not them?

I remember thinking, *Why are they staying in that stable?* They looked like such average people. I sure hope that little guy grows up to be strong and healthy. If he was who the angel said he was, maybe he will be able to do something to help people like me and my family. We sure could use it. Then it was time for me to take over my watch with the sheep. I just know I won't have any trouble staying awake tonight.

—The shepherds' story is in Luke 2:8–20.

8. We Saw It in the Heavens

I've always been interested in the heavens. The movement of the planets, the position of the moon, and the constellations intrigue me. I was taught as a boy that the gods controlled the paths of these heavenly bodies, and though I knew it was not a precise science, I knew I wanted to be an astrologer when I grew up. I learned the names of the stars and could chart the orbits of the planets so I could spot instantly when some heavenly body deviated from its normal path. It was exciting, because it gave me insight into things that were yet to happen. Reading the heavens was the best insight into the future that had yet been discovered. My parents were very pleased when I became a student at the Baghdad Astrological Institute.

I graduated with honors and was given a position where I could continue my studies with one of the leading astrologers in the country. I worked hard and rose through the ranks to become the chair of the Astrological Research Department. This position included the responsibility of charting the movements of planets, stars, and other heavenly bodies. I was required to file regular reports with the government on what these bodies told us about the life of the nation. It was a good job, and I received a lot of affirmation for what I was doing.

One day, as I was tracking the planets, I saw something in the heavens that was startling. Jupiter and Saturn were coming together in the constellation Aries, something I hadn't seen before. I called a meeting with several of my colleagues because I knew something that unusual had to be significant. We devoted most of our spare time for the next year doing research. We carefully tested every possibility before we dared publish our unanimous conclusions. Such a sign in the heavens could mean only one thing: a great king of the final days had been born in Palestine.

As soon as our academic term for that year was over, the three of us made plans to go to Palestine because we knew this was the most important discovery we'd ever make. We wanted to see this great king. When we convinced the institute of the importance of our discovery, the people there agreed to grant us a leave of absence to make the trip.

But when we got to Jerusalem, the king—a dreadfully inefficient man named Herod—didn't seem to have any idea of what we were talking about. That seemed strange. He told us, "Come back tomorrow, and we will have the information you need." We thought he would have known who in his royal family had just had a baby!

The next morning, we returned to his palace. He told us to go to a little town called Bethlehem, just south of the city, and we would find the baby we were looking for. Then he asked a question that didn't seem very important to us. He wanted to know when we had seen this special planetary conjunction. There was no reason not to tell him, so we said it had been about two years earlier. We explained it had taken us a year to gather all the data, then another six months to plan the trip and clear our teaching schedules. We couldn't understand why that was important, but you don't challenge the king when he asks a simple question, so we let it pass.

But we had a far more important concern with Herod. We knew this was a very important event, so we invited him to come with us. We assumed that this child would be a relative in some way and that he would want to see this future king. But Herod wasn't interested. He said, "No, sorry, but I'm busy. You go, find this child, and let me know where he is. I'll come later when I have more time." That surprised us, but we left Jerusalem and headed for Bethlehem.

Where do you start when you're looking for a particular child? We started asking people, "Do you know of a family that had a baby boy in the past two years?" The response was confusing. The only one people seemed to know about was a baby boy born to a young couple, Mary and Joseph. But that had been just two or three weeks earlier, not several years! They gave us directions on how to find them.

We found their little house on a narrow side street. When we knocked on the door we could tell they were genuinely surprised to see us. We explained who we were, and they invited us in. They apologized because we had to spread one of our own rugs and sit on the floor. This family had almost nothing in their house, just a mat on the floor in the corner and a little table for eating. That is hardly what we were expecting for the family of future royalty.

We told this couple about how we had seen a star, what it meant, and why we had come. Mary responded by telling us her story—how an angel had appeared to her, why they had come to Bethlehem, and the problems they had had in finding a room, and that eventually they wound up staying in a stable behind an inn. She told us how hard it had been for them. They hadn't planned on having the baby in Bethlehem, but the trip from Nazareth had been exhausting for her, and that must have induced labor. But it had all worked out. Joseph had found work as a carpenter's helper, so they were surviving, but just barely, until she was strong enough to make the trip back to Nazareth.

We stayed most of the afternoon. There was something about that time together with this young couple. It had a kind of sacred, spiritual quality to it. I'm not religious like the Jewish people are, but these two seemed to have a quiet integrity, a love for their child, and a hope for the future that had something special about it. They were so surprised when we gave them the gold, perfume, and myrrh we had brought. We had to encourage them to take it. They were embarrassed as they accepted it, but we could tell they were very grateful.

I'd never been in a house before where people lived in such poverty. They had virtually nothing, yet they weren't bitter. They believed they were going to make it. I was so glad that we had come and that we had had something to share with them, because they were so warm and open as they had shared with us. We sensed how the family was completely different from the people in King Herod's court. If this baby ever did grow up to be king, I had the distinct feeling he'd be a much better king than Herod.

I didn't sleep well that night. I had this horrible dream about soldiers running around, babies getting killed, and … and Herod laughing in the background. I woke up and couldn't get back to sleep. I was worried about this young couple we had just met. What was my dream trying to tell me?

All young couples are optimistic about their future, but what was life going to be like for these new parents? How could they have much hope with this baby living in a life of abject poverty? In my dream, Herod was always just behind a pillar or in the shadows, and he was quite a menacing figure. I knew I was reliving the conflict between how we had experienced Joseph and his wife and how we had been treated by Herod. Why hadn't he come with us? Would he do something terrible to this family? There was something about King Herod I just did not trust.

Just before the sun came up, I told my colleagues there was a change of plans. We weren't going back to King Herod. We wouldn't go to Jerusalem. We were going to head east and get out of Palestine as fast as we could. I told them about my dream. I said, "Before we go, there's one thing I have to do." I went straight to that little house we had visited the day before. They were awake when I got there, and I urged them to take their baby boy and get out of town immediately. I know it sounded strange, but I pleaded with them to go right away. I told them what I had felt with King Herod and how I was afraid of what he might do to them. I insisted that they get out of town that day, to not wait until the next day, and to not tell anyone where they were going. I suggested they get clear out of the country and go to Egypt, where they would be safe.

I gave them some money and told them there was a caravan heading for Egypt. That would be faster and much safer than traveling alone. Within the hour, they were out of the house and on their way south to Egypt. I was sorry to have frightened them so badly, but in my country, we take dreams very seriously. I couldn't shake the feeling they were in real danger, and I wasn't going to leave until I knew they were gone.

By the time I got back to my colleagues, they were ready to leave. As we traveled, I told them what I had done, and they agreed it had been the right thing to do. They had the same feelings of dread about Herod. We headed out of Palestine in the most direct way possible so as to protect ourselves from Herod's anger at not reporting back to him.

When we got home, I went back to my office, and for the next thirty years, I charted the heavens, filed my reports, met my classes, and read student papers analyzing the astrological movements in the heavens. But I thought a lot about that young family we had met in Bethlehem. We believed there was something special, something distinctly sacred about that baby boy. Was he honestly destined to grow up and become a person who would do something important with his life?

I wonder if he ever did. I wish I knew.

—The story of the wise men is in Matthew 2:1–12.

9. A Prayer Is Answered

A lifetime is a long time to wait. One day flows into the next, and after a while, you stop counting. My life began with the joy all parents have with the birth of a child. My parents were quite religious. Their lives were dedicated to the service of God as described in the Torah and taught in the synagogue. All that I remember is that I was a happy child in a loving family.

At age sixteen, I was married to a good man. Samuel was about ten years older than me, but we were happy together. He took good care of me, and life was good for us. He was a teaching rabbi in the synagogue connected with the temple in Jerusalem. I was happy to live my life as a quiet wife in support of my husband. I didn't think of it in any way other than being normal—except that I was exceptionally happy.

We wanted to have children, but that didn't happen. Perhaps it was a good thing, because after only seven years of marriage, Samuel became sick. Several months later, he died. I was a widow in a world that was not very kind to widows. That was when the temple priests suggested I come live in the temple. There were custodial rooms easily converted to living space for me. In exchange for that, I would assist in cleaning the temple so that it would always be ready for worshippers.

Some might think living in the temple would be confining, but I never saw it that way. I had security and safety; I was able to live and be present in the working space my husband had loved. It was as though I could talk with him every day as I prayed, ate, and cleaned the temple. I was still a young woman, but in a strange way, I never thought of remarrying. It was as though I was married to my life in the temple because the memories of my husband were always there as I walked through the various open spaces.

After ten years of cleaning and helping in any way I could, almost by accident I was asked to help one day as a set of parents brought their child for temple dedication. Usually, two rabbis shared in the service of dedication. One recited the biblical texts and the liturgy of dedication while the other rabbi held the baby. We found that babies were more content if they were a bit farther from the strange, masculine voice that was totally new to them. This also allowed the officiating rabbi to focus more intently on the recitations and prayers of the dedication ceremony.

One day, a couple came, and only one rabbi was present to do the dedication service. He asked me if I would hold the newborn while he recited the litany of dedication. I was thrilled. The chance to hold a newborn, even if it was someone else's newborn sent a burst of joy through my whole body. It was as close as I would ever get to actually being a mother, and my heart literally sang all through the brief dedication service. As I handed the baby back to its mother, she smiled and said, "My baby was comfortable in your arms. You like children, don't you?" I smiled and as I nodded. I had to fight back the tears of joy that I felt inside me.

I was certainly not expecting what happened the next morning. The high priest stopped me in my normal cleaning duties. "I heard about how you assisted Rabbi Ezra with the infant dedication yesterday. He was very pleased with how it went. He asked whether you could assist him again at his next dedication service. That is not normally the way we do things, but if you're willing, let's try it a few times and see how it goes. Would you be willing to help in that way?"

"Would I be willing?" I almost burst into tears on the spot. I said I would be honored and I would do my very best to help make the service meaningful for the parents and their baby. So for a week, I was there to hold each newborn child as it was dedicated to the Lord. It gave me a joy I hadn't felt since before Samuel died.

After a week, the high priest told me he'd been watching and he approved of what he saw. He would like for me to accept the task of sharing in all the dedication services that way. He suggested that I dedicate myself to fasting and praying so my service would truly be a spiritual contribution.

That was how I moved from cleaning and sweeping to fasting and praying. I had seen my former work of cleaning as a grateful gift to God, but to be sharing in the dedication of an infant and to have time for daily prayer and fasting was more than I had ever dreamed possible for me, a young woman, once a wife, now a widow.

Every time I held an infant, I tried to focus on the prayers offered for that child and for the parents. I didn't have any spoken role in these prayers, but I began to pray in my heart for each child, asking God to bless the parents and, that the child would grow to be healthy and would love God with all its heart, mind, soul, and strength. For over fifty years, I assisted in this very small way in the dedication of children in the temple.

Perhaps it's wistful dreaming, but as I got older, I began to dream about how it might be if I could hold a child who would someday grow up to be a prophet of God, or a leading rabbi.

One morning, I had the strangest experience. A young couple, Joseph and Mary were their names, brought in their first child, a baby boy they had named Jesus. She was a very young mother. With a smile, she handed me the infant child and took a step back. I caught my breath as I felt a warm glow go through me. It was as though a fire had been started deep within me. I looked at the sleeping baby boy. *This is the one!* I don't know how I knew it, but I did. A sense of wholeness swept through me. I looked at the mother. She had an adoring look in her eyes as she watched me hold her child. She knew something about this child that I did not know, yet I knew she shared exactly the same feeling I was having. All children are special to their parents—I know that—but this child was different. It was as though not only was he special to his mother and father, but he was also special to the temple, or maybe I should say to Yahweh, God of the temple.

At the end of the ceremony, I took a final look at the tiny child and handed him to his mother. I knew that I had been in the presence of God in a very special way. To this day I cannot explain it, but I knew my life was now complete. My prayer had been answered.

—The story of Anna is in Luke 2:36–38.

10. Patience with God

When you live your whole life in anticipation of something that never happens and everyone feels sorry for you, it's easy to drift into constant sadness. Everything in my family background was perfect. We had more priests in my family tree than I could name. I was told that when I was born, almost right away, everyone assumed I'd grow up and marry within the priestly tradition of Aaron. If I'd been born a boy, I would have been trained from early childhood to be a priest. That was our destiny. So being a girl, everything in my childhood was done with the purpose of preparing me to be the wife of a priest.

That meant that I was permitted to do some study in the Law and the prophets. My studies were not nearly as intensive as were the studies my brothers had. They would be priests; the closest I'd come to that was being the wife of a priest, but I knew that was an honor. I heard that over and over. "Elizabeth, you have the highest calling any woman could have. You will be the wife of a priest and the mother of his children. God will bless you."

Thus, I grew up believing I was special. But then, when I reached the traditional age for marriage, a problem arose. Twice I learned that one of the young men in our village had talked with my parents about wanting to marry me. Both times my parents refused because neither of them was from a family in the priestly tradition. At first that didn't bother me, but when I reached my mid-twenties and was still not married, I began to wonder if the blessing I had been promised might turn out to be a curse.

I will never forget the first time I saw Zechariah. He had completed his rabbinic training and was the rabbi in a village about twenty kilometers away. It was the feast of Purim, and our own rabbi was in Jerusalem, so Zechariah had come to lead our synagogue observance of this festival. Purim is not a major feast, so the attendance was small, but our family went to everything religious.

Zechariah was a good speaker, and he obviously knew the Esther story well. But the way he told it and the lessons he drew from it were creative and practical. He answered questions with tact and understanding. It was a delightful Friday evening study time. Most of the small crowd left rather quickly after the service was over. My parents were talking with Zechariah as he put the Scriptures back into their cabinet. I listened to their conversation. I joined in, as I often did, asking Zechariah why God had wanted our people to kill so many Persians in retaliation for Haman's actions against the Jews. I didn't understand why so many people had had to die.

Zechariah closed the door to the cabinet, turned to me and began to explain the situation and why the Jewish people had the right to protect themselves. Halfway through his answer, he paused and asked me what I thought might have been a better solution. I stuttered for a moment, amazed that he had actually asked for my opinion, and I told him what I thought about that dilemma in our history. It was only two or three sentences, but he leaned ever so slightly toward me and asked, "You are Elizabeth, aren't you? I hear that your family has allowed you to study the Scriptures. Now I understand why. You ask very good questions." That was all he said to me, but I remembered it.

About three months later, Zechariah was back in the synagogue, assisting in the Sabbath teaching. After the service ended, he took the initiative to stop me as I was leaving. Actually, I was walking out very slowly on purpose. He asked me a question about the evening lesson. That led to a slightly more extended conversation, and I began to hope.

It was two weeks later when my parents told me over our evening meal that Zechariah had come that day, asking their permission to talk with me about marriage.

My heart skipped six beats not only because he had come but also because of the approach he was taking. Normally, the man would ask my parents, and they would agree or not, and that would be it. But Zechariah wanted to talk to me. That was not the way we did things. My parents were smiling at my astonishment. Father said, "We told him we totally approved and we thought you would too, so we encouraged him to talk to you soon." I don't think I have ever been so happy.

Two days later, Zechariah was at the door, asking to speak with me. I know I just floated out to meet him. He explained he was impressed with my interest in the Scriptures and that I would be an excellent helper for him in his work as a priest. He told me we would never be rich but we would be happy. He wanted me to be his wife. I could hardly wait for him to stop talking so I could say *Yes!*

I learned later that he was about fifteen years older than me and that his studies had been so exciting that he hadn't had time to think about marriage. He said that he wanted to have a family and that together we would raise our children in the ways of God. It was perfect!

A year later, we were married. People from both our villages came to share in the ceremony, and everyone told us that we were meant for each other and that God certainly had good things to come in our lives. Both Zechariah and I knew that the "good things" they were talking about were children. We were ecstatically happy as we began our new life together.

The first year passed, and everything was going well, except I didn't get pregnant. Zechariah said not to worry, that there were many adjustments to be made in a marriage.

But by the fifth year, and still no children, I was terribly disappointed. While Zechariah was very understanding, I knew he was disappointed.

When twenty years went by with no children, Zechariah tried to help me feel better by talking about all the children we had to care for in the synagogue family and how we could celebrate their lives together. I appreciated his attempts, but I felt so responsible. I prayed often to become pregnant, and at times, I heard him begging God for a son. I know that many other people were also praying. I wondered sometimes what God was trying to do to me. I struggled hard to be a good wife, and Zechariah was never critical of me, and our life together was very good. If only I could have a child!

I remember the evening very well. Zechariah had come home from the synagogue, and we sat down for our evening meal. We talked about our life together and the wonderful things we had done. He told me he knew I was disappointed we hadn't had a child. He said something that had never gone through my mind. "Elizabeth, I know you feel responsible, but perhaps it is not you. Maybe it is me who can't have a son. Perhaps God is testing me, not you."

I burst into tears. Maybe I am not bad or evil. Maybe God is not angry at me. To hear my husband say that I shouldn't blame myself any longer was so kind. To be reassured that he loved me even though we hadn't had any children gave me hope again. Let's not give up trying.

Less than a week later, Zechariah told me we would be going to Jerusalem for a month. He had been given the opportunity to be priest at the temple as part of the regular rotation. He was very pleased. It was a distinct honor, and I was so happy for him.

A month later, we moved into the priests' rooms at the temple, and Zechariah began his duties. Life for us was a bit less hectic because we were living where he worked. He would stop by our rooms once or twice during the day just to tell me what he was doing. He was so excited by this opportunity. Our life together returned to the joy and excitement we had felt years before.

One afternoon, I got the surprise of my life. Zechariah came home a little later than usual, and to my amazement, he couldn't talk. Everything else was normal—he just couldn't speak. He took a board and wrote—"frantically scribbled" would be a better way of putting it—about what had happened at the temple. He had had a vision of an angel who told him I was going to have a son, and when he asked the angel a question, the angel said, "Because you did not believe me, you will be mute until the baby comes"!

I couldn't believe what he was saying—until I remembered something I wanted to tell him. My life had been so normal, and everything about me was so regular, but the last week, I had missed my period. I hadn't said anything because I wanted to be sure I wasn't just late, but it had been a week by then. I knew it was too early to say, but there was a slight chance I might be pregnant. Being late had never happened to me before. I asked him to remember that it was more than a month since we had that talk over our evening meal, and I wondered if he remembered what we had done that night and how special it had been (for me, at least). Could it be that God was answering our prayers?

We moved home at the end of Zechariah's term in Jerusalem. Five months later, my niece Mary came to visit. I was delighted to have her come, but I was shocked by her news. She told me she was pregnant. Her explanation was that she was still a virgin but that she had been visited by an angel and that her pregnancy was by the Holy Spirit. That took some getting used to, but I trusted her. She was really hurting, because Joseph, her betrothed, hadn't believed her and had rejected her. We talked and talked about it and what she could do. I don't know if I was much help, but it was good to have her with me.

I was delighted when Joseph contacted Mary. He had changed his mind and he wanted to get married as soon as possible. Mary was unbelievably happy, and I was so thankful. Mary went home and our baby came all in the same month.

We had a minor concern when the baby was born. All our friends wanted us to name him Zechariah after his father. But Zechariah and I were insistent. "His name is John." After all we had been through, we were going to follow the instructions of the angelic messenger to the jot and tittle. Nine months living with a man who couldn't talk was enough for me!

As I reflect on my life, we prayed and prayed. We waited and waited. We had made our life the best we could in those disappointing years. We were determined not to be angry at God, but sometimes, it was difficult to understand. The birth of John was a wonderful blessing. We poured all our stored-up love into him.

Now, I am an old woman. Zechariah died several years ago, and John is now a man. He is a very spiritual person, but he doesn't want to be a priest. His role models are Isaiah, Jeremiah, and Amos. I am quite content with that. He has a questioning mind, just like his father. I trust that God will find a way to use him. I continue to pray every day that his voice will be heard by many. He was such a blessing to me. I pray he will be a blessing to others.

—The story of Elizabeth is in Luke 1:5–25, 39–80.

11. Where Did This Come From?

I've been the steward for a lot of weddings. Officially, I manage the household of a very wealthy Jewish family, but we have an agreement that I can serve as the wedding steward for friends and relatives of the family. It is not an easy thing to do even though I've done hundreds of them. Every family wants things done their way, and everything has to be done just right.

This was not a big wedding, perhaps a hundred guests, and it was just a one-day event. Everything had been ordered. I always order more than needed just in case. You can never be too careful.

Things were going quite smoothly. The rabbi was just beginning to lead the couple through a very nice service when one of the servants came to me with the news every steward dreads. "Sir, have you seen the size of the crowd? We counted nearly a hundred and seventy! We don't have enough wine for that many people!"

You just can't turn people away from a wedding. You need to feed them and have wine for everyone. But we were prepared for one hundred, not one hundred seventy!

I ducked into the kitchen and sent a trusted assistant in search of more food. I had him double everything. But the wine was a different matter. I had been firm with our wine merchant and had taken virtually everything he had on hand. I whispered to the wine servers, "Go easy on the wine! Don't fill the cups. We must make what we have stretch."

That worked for a while, but by late afternoon, one server told me they were down to the last jar. Normally, you hope no one knows that, but a sister of the bride's mother heard the comment. She came over and asked if there was anything she could do. I explained we were running out of wine. If she knew where we could get more, I'd be very grateful.

She tugged on my sleeve. "Wait here. I have an idea." She turned and was gone. I saw her talking to a young man who didn't seem very happy with whatever she was telling him. But she wasn't taking his no for an answer. She brought him to me. All she said was, "He will help you. Do what he says." I referred him to my assistant and went to check on the food.

I could see out of the corner of my eye that there was a bustle of activity over by the wine table. Three servants were frantically filling empty wine casks. I couldn't see any more than that. But it made no sense. I knew there were no extra wine casks available anywhere, but there was nothing I could do about that right then.

Not long after that, one of the wine servers brought a cup of wine to me. He told me to taste it. I did, expecting it to be flat, tasteless. But it wasn't. It was of excellent vintage, and it had a beautiful sparkle. "Where did you get this?" I didn't wait for an answer. I went to the groom and asked, "Where have you been keeping this wine? I'd ordered all the wine. Where were you hiding this? This is the best wine I've tasted in years. We should have started with this wine, not the stuff we were serving."

The groom gave me a strange look. "We didn't have any wine hidden anywhere. We thought you were going to handle all the wine, like you said you would. I don't know what you're talking about."

So I went back to my assistant. "Where'd you find this wine?"

He shrugged. "We filled the five casks with water, just like he told us to, and we let it set for a brief time. Then he told me to bring a cup to you. So that's what I did."

I looked at his quizzically. "You're sure it was water you put in those wine casks?"

"Absolutely. I drew the water myself. Why?"

When we cleaned up late that evening, I wanted to taste that wine again. But I was too late. Someone had emptied the casks and filled them with water. We do that to clean out the old wine taste so the wine merchant can reuse them. But usually, that was the last step in the cleanup process. That was so the servants could get a taste of the wedding wine. I was disappointed and confused. I wanted to taste that wine again because it was some of the best I'd ever tasted. I wanted to know where it had come from. I guess I'll never know, but I was certainly relieved to have had everything work out so well.

Another thing I wondered about but never got an answer. Who was the man Mary had spoken to? The man who somehow supplied the new, really good wine? If he knew where to get that kind of wine, I wanted him as my wine merchant.

—The wedding at Cana story is told in John 2.

12. What Can A Woman Do?

I can hardly remember when I wasn't like this; it happened so long ago. I had been living a very normal life. I was an average young woman and was fortunate that my parents had accepted a marriage proposal from the parents of a young man who had even asked me about it first. We had been friends for several years, and I was thrilled when he told me he was asking his parents to talk with my parents about marriage. I was as happy as any young woman could be.

Two years into the marriage, we had a little girl, followed by a boy. Then I gradually became aware that something was wrong. I missed my regular menstrual cycle, then a second one, but I wasn't pregnant. Then my cycles became irregular and totally unpredictable until it was a never-ceasing problem.

My husband Jesse wanted to know what was wrong because he could tell I was not my normal self, and any sexual activity was just not possible. I was grateful he was so understanding. Most men would have gotten impatient.

That went on for two years. Finally, we decided to find out what was wrong and what we could do about it. The first doctor said that I should just relax and change my diet. In a few months, he said, the problem would correct itself. That visit cost us several days' pay, and it didn't work.

About a year later, I took two days, went to Jerusalem, and saw a better doctor. Jesse paid him a whole week's pay, money we couldn't afford. He told me this sometimes happens in women, and he prescribed some herbs he thought might help. They didn't.

A visit to a third doctor didn't give me any more hope, but it cost us four days' pay. When I went back to him again, he suggested a different doctor. By then I was exhausted, and my whole digestive system was giving me problems; I could hardly eat. I was tired, I was frightened, and I knew we didn't have any more money for doctors. The fourth doctor told me it was an emotional condition that had no physical connection. He suggested the same herbs the first doctor had prescribed, and he told me to abstain from any sexual activity for at least three months. I didn't tell him I'd been abstaining for three years. By then, I was ready to give up. Was this how it was going to be for the rest of my life?

You see, most people don't understand what that's like. I can't be a good wife for Jesse, and I can't go out in public because I am ritually unclean all the time. And it isn't even my fault. I have tried to solve it, but I can't. We have spent far more money on doctors than we could afford. They were quite willing to take our money, but none of them gave me any positive help. Am I condemned for the rest of my life to be who I am right now? Why should society have the right to tell me I am unclean when there is nothing I can do to change it? I had certainly tried.

My children were growing up, but I was forbidden from going with them to their synagogue school or to worship. Jesse has to go to the markets to buy food. I had no friends. I didn't want to live that way. I gradually faded back into my home and lost the joy of living.

One day, my husband told me he had heard of a prophet-rabbi named Jesus. There were rumors floating around that he had healed some people—a blind man, a leper, and a crippled man. Jesse wanted me to see if this Jesus could help me. I wasn't ready for that. Those who had been healed were all men. I was a woman. If doctors couldn't help me, how could a prophet-rabbi do anything? Besides, we had no money for any more doctors.

That was not the first time Jesse and I argued about this. I knew I was not allowed outside in mixed company---he said he'd go with me. I didn't see how anyone could help me--- he said we had to try. I told him there was no way a rabbi-teacher would pay any attention to me, that there would be a crowd around him and that he'd be too busy for me--- Jesse said I had to be more aggressive. I knew inside myself that I wanted to go. I would have tried anything at that point. But I also knew I wouldn't do it. I didn't want to have my hopes dashed again. It had been twelve years, and I was learning to live with my condition. I told Jesse it was nice of him to suggest it but I wasn't ready.

Two days later, Miriam, my best friend (actually, almost my only friend), stopped by our house all excited. This Jesus rabbi was in town, and she had seen him. He looked so friendly and talked to almost everyone. She was so excited. She stayed for only a moment before she dashed off to tell someone else. I began to cry. I had dreamed of what it would be like to be clean again. I thought about what it would mean for Jesse and our life together. What if Jesse was right and this Jesus person could help? But did I dare go out by myself? How could I get his attention? What would I say? I would be so embarrassed. I couldn't see myself doing it.

Then I got hold of myself. I couldn't sink any lower. I decided I am going to do it. I got a clean robe and started out the door and down the street before I could talk myself out of it. I saw a crowd about a hundred yards ahead of me.

I was trembling all over. How would I recognize which one was him? What if he ignored me? That was what everyone else did. I was a nobody.

I held back, afraid to get too close. But then a slight opening appeared, and I wiggled through it until I was only two or three feet from him. He was talking to several men when he turned and took a step away from where I was standing. I was so afraid! I didn't know what to do. I took a quick step, tripped, and fell to my knees. I reached out in desperation, grabbing the hem of his robe.

And then exactly what I feared most happened. He stopped, looked around, and asked, "Who touched me?" I began to cry in shame. I had failed. Not only had I failed, I had become the center of attention. Why had I come?

The men with Jesus were surprised. They wanted to know what he meant. There were lots of people around. Anyone could have bumped him. "No" he said. "Someone touched me—with purpose. I felt it."

As I lay on the ground, wishing I could just disappear, I felt a rush of fever-like warmth cascade over my body. I looked up through my tears and saw the friendliest face looking at me. He quietly asked what I wanted, and I just blurted out what my situation was, right in front of everybody! He reached down, took my hand, and lifted me to my feet. He smiled and said, "My child, trust me. You are healed of this affliction. Your courage and your faith have made you clean. Go in peace. Thank you for coming." For a moment I couldn't move. No person had treated me that way in years. He treated me as if I were clean, whole, normal.

By then, he was gone, and the crowd with him. I turned and started for my home, wondering what I had done, what he had done, and why he had reached out to me, a woman, a nobody, someone everyone else avoided?

That moment changed my life. I discovered what it was like to be whole again, to have something to offer others, to visit my friends in their homes, to take my children to synagogue school, to be a wife to my husband again. Why had he done that for me? I will never know, but I decided that day I would never turn my back on another person, especially on those who lived with difficulties. I was determined to do for others what he had done for me. For the first time in twelve years, I found myself singing as I walked down the dirt street to my house. It was like I had been born again into a new life.

—This story is in Mark 5:25–34 and Luke 8:34–43.

13. I Will Never Give Up

When I married a Jewish man, I knew there was the potential for cultural stress. But he was a good man, and we made adjustments. We lived in an area where there were both Jews and Canaanites, so my background was less of a problem. But our daughter created stress for us. At times, she erupted in totally unpredictable behavior. No one could explain what was causing it. It was inevitable; someone decided she had a demon. Once that claim was made, there was little I could do to respond to it. People tend to believe that kind of thing even when there's no proof of it. I knew she was a stressful child, but I loved her dearly and suffered unbelievably when she was going through one of her tantrums or attacks. There was nothing I could do. God knows I tried everything I could think of.

I wanted to be a good mother, but nothing worked. We were not mistreated by our neighbors; we were just ignored. We couldn't visit with friends because our daughter was disruptive in social gatherings. We tried to explain to her how we wanted her to behave, but she kept telling us, "Mommy, I can't help it. I don't want to be this way, but I just can't help it." Once, she told us she wished she were dead. That broke my heart. But I had to admit to myself, I had several times fantasized about what life might have been like if it were not for the grief she added to our lives.

I had heard stories about a rabbi who was excellent with children. They would come running up to him begging for a story, and he would stop and tell them one. I also heard he had special healing powers, and I wondered whether he might be able to help my daughter. But those thoughts lingered only for a moment, for he was a Jewish rabbi, and I was a Canaanite woman. What chance did I have that he would even consider allowing me to ask him for help? I knew what Jews thought of us Canaanites.

I tried to put this out of my mind because I knew there could be no future in it, but I couldn't. It wasn't fair that my daughter and I should have to suffer because we were born in a certain place. The Jewish God was certainly bigger than that. My husband had told me that many times.

One day, the town gossip was all about this rabbi who was going to be in town the next afternoon. I tried to dismiss the idea, but I finally decided I had nothing to lose. I took my daughter, praying that the demon wouldn't attack her that day. We went looking for the rabbi Jesus.

We found him with a small crowd of men gathered around him. There was no way I could get close, so I took a deep breath and cried out, "My Lord, Son of David, have mercy on me." No one paid any attention, so I shouted still louder, "Have mercy on me, Lord, Son of David." Several of the men in the group frowned at me, but I had come too far to quit that easily. One more deep breath, and I screamed at the top of my voice, "Have mercy on me, Lord, Son of David. Hear my prayer. My daughter is tormented by a demon. Please help me."

You can imagine the despair I felt when I heard the men tell the rabbi to pay no attention, that I was just a Canaanite troublemaker. They tried to get me to stop, but I wouldn't. Then I heard him say, "I cannot help everyone. I was sent to be a voice of truth and love to the house of Israel." My heart sank. It was like a dagger had been plunged into my soul.

I seized the moment and forced my way through the men until I was standing face-to-face with him. "Lord, please help me." He didn't seem to hear me. His reply was what I had heard many times: "It is not fair to take food from children to feed the dogs." I knew instantly what he meant because I'd heard that language used against me before, but this time, I wasn't going to allow it. "That is true," I said, "but even dogs get fed crumbs from the table of the children. Please help me. I know you can."

He stopped and took a step toward me. "Your faith and persistence are remarkable. You are right in what you have said. What you are asking for, you shall have. Your daughter is well."

I stood there in silence. I had done it. I never thought I would have the courage, but I'd done it. He said my daughter was well. A moment earlier, I'd been screaming at the top of my lungs, but now I was speechless.

Jesus started moving away, but he smiled as he looked back at me. It was as though he knew he had met his match. But he looked like he had enjoyed the challenge. I grabbed my daughter's hand, and we started running home.

As we slowed down to a walk, my daughter said, "Mommy, I have never seen you do anything like that before. You yelled at that man. You have never yelled at me like that. What were you doing?"

I stopped and gave her a big hug. "For you, my dear, I will yell, I will scream, and I will never quit. We are now going to start living all over again."

I committed myself to going one day at a time. I didn't know what to expect. The man said she was well, but I wondered how he'd known that. How would I know? He hadn't even touched her; he just said it. But something inside me gave me a lot of hope.

Days stretched into weeks, then months, but my daughter never had another episode of whatever it was that was bothering her.

That Jewish prophet responded to me, a Canaanite woman. He heard me. I will never forget that, and I will always be grateful. How I wish the whole world could be that way.

—The story of the Canaanite woman is in Matthew 15:21–28 and Mark 7:24–30.

14. Caught? Or Framed?

Living as the only daughter in a family with four brothers, I was quite comfortable being around boys. My brothers and I played together, and I learned to compete with them and be more independent than most young girls. My brothers were pretty typical brothers. They had rights and privileges I didn't have, but I learned to take care of myself.

When I was fifteen, my parents told me that Joel, a young man in the village, had asked them if I would be his wife. Joel was a nice man, and he was from a good family. I knew him but not well. Anyway, that was set, and I was to get married later that year.

It was a good year. We spent time together and learned to know each other better. Both our families were poor, but that meant we each knew what was ahead for us, and we were determined to have a good life.

We were married in a very nice ceremony, and everyone said it was a good marriage and wished us well. It was a good marriage. We didn't have much, but together we were making it work.

During that first year, I became pregnant, much to the delight of both of us. The birth of our daughter was a wonderful event. At about that time, Joel and I moved from our small town to Jerusalem, where he had found a good job. We felt our future would be better. Moving from the security of our families was hard, but it seemed the right thing to do.

About two years later, both my parents died of extended illnesses. It was unusual to lose two parents in the same year, but we adjusted to it. Our daughter was growing, and life was good. But then, my husband died in an accident at work, and suddenly I was left alone with a three-year-old daughter. I had no skills that would enable me to find work, my parents were both gone, and I was alone in the big city with few friends.

Not long after my husband's death, a man who had worked with him came to visit me. He expressed concern about how I was managing and wondered if he could be of help. He seemed like a nice man, and I thanked him for his concern.

Two weeks later, he was back again, but this time, things were different. After again expressing concern for me, he forced me into our back room and demanded I give him sex. I refused. He picked me up, threw me on the matt, and raped me. When he was finished, he got dressed, tossed a shekel on the floor, and told me I was good.

I lay there crying for over an hour. Sex with my husband had always been a shared event; he had always been tender and loving. But being raped was harsh, painful. I felt abused and violated. But the thing that hurt most was I knew there was nothing I could do about it. I had no parents and no friends I could talk with, so I kept it to myself and vowed to survive.

I had been put on the list to receive food baskets from the synagogue. That was enough to barely keep me and my daughter alive. I found some work doing washing in prosperous Jewish homes. It was hard work, and there was never enough money, but my daughter and I stayed alive.

I would go home each evening and be afraid. In our culture, a young woman living alone had no one to protect her. What would I do if that man came back? How could I defend myself? I tried to sleep, but I had nightmares of men coming through the door, looking in my windows. Even when I was fully dressed, I felt naked as I walked in public.

Two weeks later, the man came back again. This time, he didn't express any concern, and even though I pleaded and begged and cried, he carried me into the bedroom, and we had sex. Rather, he had sex. I felt like a detached thing he was using. As he left, once again he threw a shekel on the floor.

My nightmares stopped, but that was because I couldn't sleep. To sleep was to invite terror into my mind. I was afraid to be with people because I didn't feel safe in the same room with any man. I was afraid to be alone because I knew I didn't have the physical strength to defend myself.

It was about ten days later that another man who had worked with Joel came to my tiny home. He didn't express any concern for me; he simply put two shekels on the table, grabbed me, and dragged me into the bedroom, where he forced me into sex. When he left, he thanked me and said he'd would be back next week.

He came back, again left two shekels (more than two days' pay doing washing)—and he forced me to have sex again. As he left, he told me he was going to recommend me to a friend who would pay much more than he could. I couldn't believe what I was hearing. Was that what I was becoming? Where could I turn? What could I do?

Three days later, another man came to my door. I told him I was not available and that I would not let him into my house. He said, "That's not what my friend told me. I'm coming in." He forced his way into my house, then forced his way into me while I just lay there. When he left, he put five shekels on the table. He told me I was worth it!

Later that week, a well-dressed older man came to my door and simply walked past me when I opened it. He put five shekels on the table and pushed me into the bedroom. There was something different about him. He carefully took my clothes off and motioned for me to lie down. He took his clothes off and just lay on top of me. Right at that moment, three men burst into the room. They told the first man to take his clothes and get out. It was almost as though he'd been expecting them. The three men threw my robe at me and pulled me out of the house. I was trying to cover myself as best I could when they threw me down on the ground in front of a crowd. I was absolutely terrified and humiliated. I just lay there, trying to wrap my robe around me.

One of the men pointed at me and said, "Master, we caught this woman committing adultery with a man. The law says we should stone her. Do you agree?" My eyes went wide open. They wanted to kill me for something a man had done to me! What would happen to me? What about my daughter? How did these men know what was happening? Had they planned this? I was afraid I was going to die.

The man they were talking to was clearly embarrassed. He turned his back on them and knelt down, sort of writing in the dust. After a moment, he stood up, turned to them, and rather forcefully said, "If there is any one of you here who is so perfect that you have never made a mistake—you throw the first stone." And with that, he knelt down beside me and pulled my robe down to cover my legs. In that instant, I felt a surge of hope go through me. Maybe I would live to see my daughter again.

It was deathly quiet for a few minutes. I could sense people were leaving. The man turned to me and said, "It doesn't look like anyone here is ready to condemn you." I looked around and replied, "I don't see anyone either—except you." His response was very soft. "I am not going to condemn you. This was not your doing. But I urge you to find a way to be sure they cannot do this to you again. Don't let others force you down that road. It leads to a dead end. You're much better than that."

With that, he walked away. I sat there by myself as I watched him leave. I thought to myself: "That man was honest, and he is right. I will not to let anyone do that to me ever again. I will find a new place to live. I will ask the people where I do washing if they could help me find more work. I am going to be a good mother for my daughter. I will not let others determine who I am.

I know how my parents raised me. I am going to be a person they would be proud of. I got to my feet, wrapped my robe around me and went back to my house. I have a daughter who needs me.

—The story of this woman is in John 8:1–11.

15. I Should Have Been a Boy

Is it so wrong for someone to rather read a book than cook dinner? If you expect me to read a cookbook, why can't I read the Torah? The Torah is the center of our faith, so why shouldn't I be allowed to know what was in it and talk about it in public? My brother Lazarus, even though he was younger than me, got all the breaks. He went to synagogue school; he and Father would talk after supper about this teaching or that lesson. When I asked if I could just listen, they told me, "No. The Torah is not for girls." That never made sense. I had to obey what the Torah said, but I wasn't allowed to know what was in it? That wasn't fair.

Our family was unusual because neither Martha nor I ever got married. She remained single because no family had ever tried to arrange a marriage for her, and I had pleaded with Father not to force me into a marriage when I really had no interest. So when our parents died, Martha and I simply kept on with the family shop and continued to live by ourselves. Most of the time, we got along very well together, but sometimes, I had no interest in Martha's incessant concern about food and tidiness around the house. I know there were many times when I had curled up with a book after the shop had closed and had no idea how the evening meal made it to the table.

But that was our life, and it was a good life. Lazarus rather freely shared with me about things in the Torah, issues in the village, and new religious ideas. Thus, we talked often about a new rabbi. Well, he wasn't officially a rabbi, but he was quite a teacher with exciting insights into the Torah who was causing quite a stir around Jerusalem. Lazarus had been to hear him several times, and several times, Jesus had come home with Lazarus simply to rest, to visit, and to have supper with us.

The times with Jesus in our house were the best. He wasn't afraid to talk with women. He even used women in the stories he told. I especially like one he told about the woman who was being mistreated by a judge, and she just wouldn't take "No" for an answer. He even told stories that implied women had an important role in God's new way of living. It seemed to me like he was saying, "Mary, the kingdom of God is for women like you too." That was good news. And it wasn't only me; other women in Bethany said they felt the same way. Jesus treated them like human beings, important people. He wasn't afraid to be seen talking with women even though some men said he was a bit too free in the way he included women in his circle.

Anyway, we had a tense time at our house one evening. Lazarus told Martha and me that Jesus, Peter, James, and John were in town, and he had invited them for supper the following day. I thought that was great. We could have a wonderful evening of conversation. Martha, however, worried about how we'd get all the food prepared for seven of us. I had suggested that all we needed was a good bowl of soup. The important thing was not the food but the time we would have to talk together. Martha, however wouldn't hear of it. We had to have meat, we had to have bread, we had to have a good wine, and a salad, and fresh vegetables, on and on. At that point, I simply walked away because I knew she had already decided and there was no use talking about it.

Sure enough, she left the shop early to get started on supper. By the time I got home after closing up, Jesus and his three friends were already there, visiting with Lazarus. I didn't want to miss anything, so I simply put my things down, went in, and sat down with the men to join in the conversation. After all, it was as much my house as it was hers.

I could hear Martha rattling pots out in the cooking area. I noticed it because she didn't usually make that much noise in the kitchen. And then I heard her clearing her throat in the doorway. I tried to ignore her, and she went back to the kitchen. But a few minutes later, right when we were having an intense exchange about what the Torah really meant when it talked about justice and fair treatment of people, Martha was back. This time she was irritated, and her voice showed it. "Jesus," she said, "I need Mary's help out here in the kitchen or we will never eat tonight. Would you please excuse her from this *discussion* so I can have some help with supper?"

I cringed at her tone. I'd heard it before. That wasn't the first time she had made it clear I spent too much time reading and talking and not enough time helping around the house. I was just starting to shift my feet under me so I could get up when Jesus responded. I could not believe what he said. "Martha, don't worry about supper. We can wait. Mary is clearly interested in the things of God, and I don't want to deprive her of that experience. What she's doing is really a good thing. We can eat later. That will be okay with us."

Wow! With that one comment, years of women being silenced got pushed off to the side. He had just told me I was a person of value. He believed what I thought and said was important. Only a woman could understand the immense feeling of joy and acceptance and wholeness that swept over me. I was a person whose ideas and thoughts actually mattered! Was that really what Jesus was saying the kingdom of God was all about? If it was, I wanted in, because that was wonderful news.

Supper was only about thirty minutes late, and Martha, as always, had prepared a simple yet elegant meal. We all complimented her on it. I noticed that when we continued our conversation about the Torah around the table, Jesus made a point of asking Martha what she thought.

That evening, as I helped Martha clean up, I told her I would try to be more help in the kitchen after this. You know what she said to me? "I really enjoyed that conversation around the table. It was nice when Jesus asked me what I thought. Most men don't do that. We should tell Lazarus to invite them again."

Something happened to both of us that night, and we knew it. Jesus came back rather often, and Martha served soup. And both of us spent more time talking with Jesus about his vision for how God's people reached out and included everyone in the circle of faith.

I have thought about that evening many times. On that night, I discovered I didn't have to be a man. I could be me, a woman, and be respected and honored and invited to share in the conversation. That was a wonderful feeling, and I am thankful Jesus made such a difference in my life.

—The story of Mary and Martha is in Luke 10:38–42.

16. I Could Use Some Help Here!

I was the oldest in the family, and they always say the oldest is the most responsible. I know it worked that way in our family. Our parents had a small sewing business in a room we had added to the house years ago. It was a good business, and while we weren't rich, we lived more comfortably than did many families in Bethany. We were close enough to Jerusalem to draw business from the city, and my parents insisted on quality work. I think that was where I learned it. I started working in the sewing shop at an early age, and I enjoyed it.

One of my earliest daily tasks was to clean up after a project was finished. I liked doing that. I liked seeing the shop as neat as a pin when I was done cleaning. I guess that is where I developed my desire for cleanliness in the house too. That was certainly not like my little sister, Mary. She would lay her things down, and that is where they would stay. She could walk through a mess and never see it. Mary never took any interest in the shop, at least not when our parents were running it. All Mary wanted to do was read.

I don't know how it happened, but one day, I thought "I am nearly thirty and not married", so I resigned myself to being single, and I devoted my creative energy to working in the shop. After our parents died, Mary got more involved, and we were able to maintain the reputation built by our parents. But I never would have asked Mary to clean up the shop. It was just so much easier if I did it myself. I would have liked it if Mary had taken a more active, helping role in cleaning the house and cooking, but that just wasn't how Mary was. She was excellent in the shop, but at home, she preferred reading and thinking rather than cooking and cleaning, so we drifted into a pattern that worked rather well for both of us.

One day, our brother Lazarus came home quite excited. He had always had a special interest in the Torah, so I wasn't surprised when he told us of a new teacher/prophet who was going around the countryside. He said the man was a follower of John the Baptist and was calling for sweeping renewal. I told him to invite him for a meal, that we would be glad to meet him.

That started one of the most exciting friendships Mary, Lazarus, and I ever had. This prophet, Jesus, had a group of disciples, and while we were not in that inner circle, Jesus often came to our house when he was near Jerusalem. He was always welcome for meals. He occasionally stayed overnight or simply dropped in to have a place to rest for a few hours. We became very good friends, and we supported what he was doing in any way we could.

One day, Lazarus told us that Jesus, Peter, James, and John would be coming for supper the next night. That wasn't a problem; that often happened. It just meant that I'd leave the shop early to work on the meal. Mary would close up.

But that day, things got hectic. We were busy in the shop, and I didn't get away as early as I had hoped. So I was just starting the food preparation when our guests arrived. Lazarus was home, so they were soon talking about some intricacies in the Torah on how to treat strangers. Soon after that, Mary came home, and I was glad to see her because I really needed her help, as I'd told her earlier that day.

But you know what she did? She came in the door, put down all her stuff on the floor, went right into the front room, and joined in the conversation with Jesus. That irritated me a bit, so I went to the doorway and tried to get her attention without interrupting the conversation. But she deliberately ignored me. Ten minutes later, I tried again. That time, I got her attention, but she still didn't move. I stood there, frowning at her, but that did no good.

I was getting desperate. I went back a third time, and during a slight break in the conversation, I got Jesus' attention and told him as politely as I could that if we wanted to eat before dark, I needed Mary to come help. I told him I didn't want to be rude, but would it be okay with him if Mary excused herself and came to help me?

I didn't expect what I got in return. Jesus said, "Our conversation is more important than supper, and it won't matter if it's late. We aren't hungry yet. Mary has a deep interest in what we're talking about."

Well, I never! I didn't know what to say, so I went back to the kitchen. Supper was about thirty minutes late, the salad was a bit wilted, the bread wasn't warm, and the meat was overcooked. Everybody said they liked it, but I knew it could have been better.

But an interesting thing happened during the meal. The group continued their conversation, and I found it interesting. I was really taken aback when Jesus asked me what I thought about including other people. I sort of stammered, but I had thought about that because of the people we met in the shop, and so I told him what I thought. He seemed genuinely interested, and he asked me to say a bit more, so I did. Others picked up on what I had said, and John specifically asked what I would do in a particular situation. It was one of the most interesting evenings I'd had in a long time. Suddenly, I understood why Mary found these times with Jesus so interesting. He treated me with respect, showed interest in what I thought, and gave me a sense of importance that a woman rarely got from men.

That evening was a big step forward for me. As we were cleaning up, I apologized to Mary for interrupting their conversation, and she said she'd try to be more helpful in the future. I also decided that when Jesus came again, we could get along quite well with just some bread and a bowl of good soup. That way, all of us could be together and talk.

I think I changed a bit that evening. I still want to have a clean house, and I still think a good meal is important. But I found out how good it feels to be included in a mature conversation about the Torah and how affirming it is when another person picks up on something you said rather than just letting it drop because you are just a woman. I found a sense of personal worth, and I liked it.

No, I didn't become a radically new person, but I did learn to feel better about myself and my ideas, and I learned it is good to share ideas with other people. I think Jesus opened a new door in my life, and I am grateful.

—The story of Martha and Mary is in Luke 10:38–42.

17. Where Can I Worship?

Growing up in my little town, I had lots of girlfriends. We did all the usual stuff—you know, playing games, staying overnight together, learning to cook and clean—everything girls were expected to do. Everybody knew everybody. It was a safe little town, and we thought life was good.

Everyone thought it was perfectly normal that when I was fifteen, my parents arranged a marriage for me with Aaron, who was twenty-two. I was pleased with the arrangement because he was a nice young man. The marriage was the usual daylong celebration; everyone wished us well, the rabbi said all the right prayers, and our life together was off to a good start.

We had four exciting, wonderful years, but then things began to get tense between us. I knew he loved me, but I also knew he was expecting me to get pregnant and was wondering what was wrong with me. I didn't know either, but you can't just *will* yourself to get pregnant.

After six years and no baby, he told me he was invoking an ancient law that permitted him to end our marriage and take a new wife. Obviously, I didn't like it, but I had no choice; it was the man's decision. So my marriage ended. That ancient law also said my husband had to provide for me, but I knew that wasn't going to happen, so I moved back with my parents.

Less than a year later, my parents told me Nathaniel had asked them if he could take me as his wife, and they had agreed. It was also a good choice for me, and while I still missed Aaron, I was determined to make this marriage work.

Three years later, I still was not pregnant, and Nathaniel explained to me he had to have a son, so he was asking the priest to get him out of the marriage. What was I to do?

After Nathanial came David, and the end result was the same—still no pregnancy. That marriage ended, as did my next one with Seth after three years. I was in my mid-thirties, and life had become a miserable strain. My parents were now quite old, and I knew I couldn't count on them to take care of me much longer. So when Peter, a thirty-five-year-old man whose wife had died several years ago talked with me, I listened. He had a very unusual idea.

He told me he would take me into his house and we would live as husband and wife, only we wouldn't get married—not just then. He said that as soon as I got pregnant—and not before—we would immediately go to the priest and get married. He said that, as he saw it, that would simplify so many things.

I didn't like the idea and told him so. But he told me to think about it for a few weeks. He promised he'd be a good husband and would provide for me; we just wouldn't get married until I got pregnant. I'd never given up hope of having a child, so I finally agreed and moved in with him.

We both knew it would happen; the town gossips erupted. But Peter said, "Don't listen to them. We'll be okay." But my life changed dramatically. I had four ex-husbands, each of whom had remarried and were raising their own families. The women in town refused to associate with me, and I heard some of the names they used to refer to me when I wasn't around. I had stopped going to synagogue, but I still prayed quietly at home. I changed my patterns for going to market and for fetching water. I knew when the other women did these things, so I waited until they had returned home before I went to the well for water. It was not how I imagined life would be, but I had food, clothing, and a place to live. Peter was certainly kind to me, but I lived with a lot of pressure and very few friends.

It was just before noon on a very average day when, as I always did, I went to Jacob's well for water. It was hot at that time of day, but I'd gotten used to that. The heat was easier to handle than the shunning I received from the other women. I was surprised to see a man sitting at the well, but he was not in the way, so I began pulling up a bucket of water.

But then he asked me if he could have a drink. I wasn't expecting that because he was clearly Jewish and I was Samaritan. I said, "You people don't talk to people like me. You know that." He sort of smiled and said, "I know, but not all of us are like that. If you knew who you are talking to, you would ask a different question."

Well, that started a conversation. You know my background. I'd had a lot of experience dealing with different men. He wanted to talk about water, so I told him that if he could help me get water without coming up here every day, I'd certainly listen. He asked about my husband. I quietly told him that I didn't have a husband, which technically was true, since Peter and I weren't married. He responded as though he was sorry. "I know. I've heard about your situation."

I wondered how he could have known that, but I changed the subject. Since he was Jewish, and he seemed intelligent, I asked him how he felt about us Samaritans since we couldn't worship in Jerusalem but had to go to Mount

Gerizim. I wondered what that meant for somebody like me. I was surprised by his answer. "I know why you can't go to Jerusalem to worship. You are a Samaritan. And I think I understand why you don't go to Mount Gerizim either. You have four husbands who probably go there every Sabbath. Woman, trust me, going to worship every week is not God's highest priority. What God wants is for people to worship with integrity, and by that, I mean by the way they think and the way they live and treat people. True worship is a living experience, not a ritual that has no connection with your life."

I was impressed with his answer, but I also felt intimidated. I told him I was looking for the Messiah to come, and while what he said made sense, I would have felt better about it if I'd heard it from the Messiah, not just another Jewish man. His answer literally made me shiver. "Woman, you are talking to your Messiah right now."

Just as he said that, a whole bunch of other Jewish men showed up, and they acted like they knew him, so I turned and left. I wasn't comfortable around that many men.

I hurried back to the village and met a cluster of women. Without thinking, I told them they should go to the well, the Messiah was there, and I had talked with him. "He knows about my life, and he understands it," I said.

Then I saw a couple of men, and I told them the same thing. I was amazed—they took me seriously. Some of them went to the well to see for themselves. They even asked him to stay for a couple of days, and much to our amazement, he did. He told us a lot of good things about God, and what God wants, and how being a Samaritan was not a bad thing. He said God loves us every bit as much as He loves the Jewish people. He talked about accepting people and not being so quick to judge others.

Those two or three days changed my life. Several of my former women friends came to visit me. They told me that they thought they knew why my former husbands had left me but that they'd been afraid to say anything because their husbands wouldn't have approved. They didn't think what had happened to me was right, and they were sorry. I was stunned when three of them asked me to come over to their houses the next day because they wanted me to tell them about what had happened at the well a few days earlier.

A lot of people in town had listened to Jesus and were impressed with what he had said. More and more often, women would stop and thank me for coming back to the village and getting Jesus to stay a few days. They hoped that life would be better for us all.

A few of the men wanted to make sure I knew I shouldn't take any credit for the changes happening in the village. They were clear. It wasn't because of what I had said but because of what Jesus had said that made the difference. I was supposed to stay in my place.

I heard them, but I was already discovering that most of the people who believed in Jesus—at least their wives—started treating me differently, and I was gradually being accepted by more and more of the townsfolk. Some of the women even invited me to go with them in the morning to get water. I began to relax for the first time in years. Maybe, just maybe, I might even get pregnant. That would truly be a miracle, but one can always believe.

—The story of the woman at the well is told in John 4:1–42.

18. When You Really Need Help

I was a very fortunate young woman. When I was fifteen, my parents arranged a marriage for me with one of the nicest young men in the village. I knew he had watched me as a young girl, but I knew better than to hope I might someday be his wife. We were both thrilled when my parents approved of the marriage. We were married a year later, and everyone in our little village of Nain knew ours would be a marriage that worked.

Life was good for over twenty-five years. My husband was a hard worker. We didn't have much, but we always had food and a place to live. Even more important, we had each other. We also had a young son who was the love of our life. He was energetic and smart. He was our hope for the future.

When David was fifteen, tragedy struck. My husband, Aaron, got sick and died within a few months. I grieved that loss for over two years. Aaron was much more than I had ever dreamed a husband could be. He had provided for us and had loved us. We were a team in a small town where many wives weren't treated very well. I didn't know how I was going to survive my loss, but David promised me he would always be there to keep things going. And sure enough, with his help, we survived, and life was getting back to normal. That is, if being a single mother could ever be described as normal.

When David turned twenty, he talked with me about getting married to Sarah, a young woman in our village. I was very pleased, and I talked with Sarah's parents, who immediately and eagerly gave their approval. Those were wonderful days, and my trust in God was starting to return.

But then—and I can hardly dare let myself think back to those days— David died after only two weeks of being sick with something no one could explain. He just lost his strength and died. I can still see Sarah's face when I told her David was gone. We just held each other and cried and cried. Life could be so unfair. It was enough to make me wonder if I was living under a curse. Sarah assured me that she had promised herself to David, and she would keep that promise with me. She would stay with me, and somehow we would get through this. But I knew the pain she was living with. I'd been through that only four years earlier, and I wondered if I had the strength or the will to go on.

But life doesn't always give you that choice. Life goes on, and you must go on with it. So we did all the necessary planning for the funeral. That walk behind David's body was even worse than the walk behind Aaron's. I felt my life had come to an end. Within five years, I had lost my husband and my son. I was alone in a world that was not kind to widows with no children. I knew I should not be angry with God, but I simply couldn't help it. The rabbis had always told us to trust in God and God would supply all our needs. I wanted to trust, but I didn't know how to do that anymore. I hoped God would understand that my pain was far more than I could bear.

It was so good to have Sarah walk beside me; I would not have made it otherwise. We were just coming out of the town gate. The cemetery was only a few hundred steps away. I wanted to stop walking and just hope that somehow David wouldn't be dead any more. I knew that wouldn't happen, but I could not face the reality of this day.

It was at that moment when a kind-looking man came out of the crowd and fell in step with me. "Don't cry," he said. I stopped to look at him. He wasn't being insensitive or casual. What I saw in his face was a pain that came close to matching my own. He walked over to the bier. Everyone stopped moving. We just watched. He reached out and touched David's body. That in itself was different. We Jewish people avoid touching dead bodies whenever we can. Quietly he said, "David, your mother needs you here. Get up!"

I don't know what I was expecting, but it certainly wasn't what I got. Had God heard my prayer of five minutes ago? Did God still care about me? David was sitting up. He looked a bit confused and asked what everyone was doing there. Had someone died that he didn't know about?

Then he saw Sarah and reached out his hand to her. I never saw a person move as fast as she did. In less than half an instant she was at his side with tears streaming down her face in sheer, unbelievable joy. David responded by standing up, and breaking almost every rule of Jewish etiquette, he wrapped his arms around her and held her. In public!

Jesus looked at me with an almost mischievous smile on his face as he said, "Mother, maybe you should welcome your son back home. He has been on a short journey. He is glad to see you, too!"

The response of the crowd was wonderful. They were amazed and almost instantly thanked God for what they had just seen. And you know, for several years, almost everywhere I went, people would stop me and say, "We heard about your son. We are so happy for you. It is truly a sign for all of us that God still cares about us."

—This widow's story is in Luke 7:11–17.

19. So This Is What the World Looks Like!

I first met Simon when we were young boys. We were both blind, and that meant we had few friends. Yes, there were those who had known us from birth and knew our families, but when you are blind, it's hard to have casual acquaintances. People don't know how to treat you or how to respond to you in a conversation. What do you tell people when they want to talk very loudly to you because you're blind? Do they think we hear with our eyes? Did you ever notice how much people use their hands when they talk? I've never seen that, of course, but I knew when they were doing that because I could hear it in the language they used: "Come here … Get that box over there … It is this big." Where is "here", and how small is "this big"? You get the idea.

Simon and I became close friends. We played games together. Yes, blind people play games—just different games. We shared the knowledge we picked up as we listened to people talk on the street. We knew exactly where to go to receive good treatment in the small shops and when to go there so it wouldn't be crowded. It was nice to have a friend who understands you, because in our town, most people didn't. Even the religious community intentionally avoided us.

We knew we were not allowed inside the temple for worship, but we could sit outside and hear what was being read. Being outside was sort of like being inside because we couldn't see any better inside than we could outside, so it didn't make much difference. But no matter how hard we tried to help, it was difficult for our parents. We had learned to function quite well, and there were even places where we could find special jobs, but they were irregular and not dependable.

One day, we were told Jesus was in town. A friend promised to take us to hear him. That was truly exciting. When you are blind, you learn how to see with your ears, and as we listened to Jesus, we "saw" a kind, sensitive, and patient person, the type of person you could talk to.

About two months later, Jesus was back. I was determined to ask Jesus to help us. But Simon wasn't sure. Why would Jesus pay any attention to us? We'd been blind forever, so how could we believe he could change that? But I was stubborn, so he finally agreed to come with me. We knew the streets well. As we went to where Jesus would pass by, we whispered to each other.

"Let's talk to him."

"But what will we say?"

"Let's ask him to heal our blindness."

"Would he do that? Do you think he really would?"

"I don't know, but at least we can ask."

"Okay, you ask him. What will you say? You can't just walk up and say, 'Heal me'!"

I decided we'd get as close to the road as we could. We would sit down and simply cry out for mercy. That wouldn't be making any demands, and Jesus could do whatever he chose. When I heard the crowd coming, I cried out, "Have mercy on me, Son of David. Please have mercy on me." Simon joined in. Some of the people standing around us told us to be quiet, but we weren't about to be silenced now. We had to shout a couple of times before Jesus turned and asked, "Do you really think I can heal you?"

That put me on the spot. I wasn't exactly sure what I expected. I know I sort of stammered and said, "Yes I do. I think you can if you will only do it." I hoped that was an appropriate answer. That was why we were there, but I didn't want to sound like we were demanding anything.

I could feel the closeness of his hands as he touched my eyes. It was a strong but a very tender, almost loving touch. Those fingers could never hurt anyone, I could tell. I heard him pray, something like, "Father, you know the life of this man and what he has to live with every day. I know you want all people to see the truth and live in the beauty of your creation, so help him see so he can praise you."

He took his hands off my eyes, and I squinted in the bright sunlight. I saw things I had never seen before, beautiful things that people had told me about, like trees, and people's faces. I saw birds that I had heard many times (So that is what they looked like). People say, "I just can't believe my eyes." Well I could, because I'd heard, or I had felt, or I had sensed all these things, but to see them in living color? It was far more beautiful than anything I'd ever imagined.

I looked at Simon. Tears were streaming down his face. Not just an occasional tear. A torrent of tears. His expression was one of absolute amazement and gratitude. I spoke for both of us as I fell to my knees.

Jesus said to me, "It's a beautiful world, isn't it? But listen carefully. I don't want you telling anyone how this happened. That will be just between the three of us, understand?"

Without thinking, I blurted out, "Yeah, sure,whatever you say." And with that we left.

But in the excitement of seeing everything for the first time, Simon and I started going up to strangers on the street, pointing out things we could see, and explaining what had happened to us. I told my family and then my friends. How could I possibly keep my mouth shut when suddenly I was doing something I'd never done before, like seeing a tree, a dog, a child, a cloud? Even the mud we were walking on was so interesting to finally see! It wasn't long before almost everyone in our village knew about what had happened to us. I told the story a hundred times, sometimes two or three times to the same person. When you are seeing the world for the first time, you have a lot to talk about. And no one should ever tell you to keep quiet.

—The story of the blind men is in Matthew 20:29–34.

20. One of the Ten

I was the oldest of three children in my family. My siblings and I enjoyed the normal things children did. We played together, did our synagogue studies together, and helped our parents as much as we could. I had heard about leprosy, but it was always far away and shadowed in mystery. No one in our town even knew anyone with that dreaded, incurable disease.

I don't remember exactly when I started to feel weakness in my legs and the loss of energy over my whole body. I thought it was just fatigue and perhaps a light fever I had picked up, something that I had simply lived with until it went away. Little did I know I would be living with this the rest of my life—if you can call what I had "a life".

No one in our family thought much about it until several months later. I never fully recovered, when my skin began to break out in blisters and rashes. It felt awful, and nothing helped. It was then that the local priest first used the word *leprosy*. You'd never believe the instant impact that one simple word could have on you. That very same day everything I had in the house was taken outside, a tent was pitched for me behind our small house, and my mother could not stop weeping.

The priest informed them the next day of a leper colony about two days' journey away, and he arranged for me to move to that death-sentence colony that was to be home for the rest of my life. The sad thing was that it wasn't actually a death sentence; it was much worse. I was now listed among the living dead in the minds of most people. I could not even give my siblings or my parents good-bye hugs. I know that hurt my mother, but father would not permit it. And he was right in doing that. I know he hated saying that to Mother because he also was crying, and I know he was hurting as much as I was.

I told them I wanted to walk; and I wanted to walk by myself. There was something inside me that was trying to make me believe that if I delayed arriving at the colony, maybe I wouldn't have leprosy by the time I got there. That was hard for a twenty-year-old who only two days ago had his whole life ahead of him. Now there was no reason to live.

There were about twenty people in the *colony*. I hate using that word because it was simply a cluster of mud huts with virtually no semblance of meaningful life. Why would you expect anything better when you know this is simply where you have been sent to die before you have the chance to infect anyone else?

We fended for ourselves. We grew our own food, had water brought to the edge of the compound each day. Going into the village was allowed, but after two or three times, I decided it wasn't worth the pain I felt. People gave us a wide berth, avoiding any kind of contact, and we were required by law to identify ourselves as lepers if anyone approached us. No one ever saw me as a person again. I had become an unnamed leper, and everyone else was thankful they were not me.

But you know, you can get used to being a nonperson if you do it long enough. We developed a tiny bit of community within our own group, but even there, having leprosy really isolated you from other lepers, and it could even isolate you from yourself.

When I left home, my mother promised she would send food and stay in touch with me. That is an odd phrase—"Stay in touch." She and I both knew that would never happen, and yet I knew exactly what she wanted to do.

About once a month, one of my siblings would come with some food, even a little bit of money, but after several years, even those visits got further and further apart. I don't remember when anyone from my family had visited me last. I didn't blame them. If the situation had been reversed, I didn't know if I would want to come near this place either.

But even in our colony, we occasionally got word about what was going on in the world around us. Probably the best part was that the Roman army also left us alone. But one day, an uncle of one of my friends told us about a traveling rabbi who was causing quite a stir. There were rumors going around about some people who had been healed; a blind man, and even a lame man. It was exciting news for a couple of days, but then reality hit me. What were the chances of any rabbi ever coming to our place? Even rabbis kept their distance. And nobody was ever healed of leprosy, so what could he do? On top of that, we were told he traveled with a group of twelve men and a couple of women and were almost always surrounded by a small crowd. Even if we tried, there'd be no way we would be allowed to get anywhere near him. So I tried to get him out of my mind because it was just not going to happen. I actually did forget about him. You can force yourself to forget about things when you have no hope.

But one of our group brought up the subject one morning. He had heard that this rabbi, named Jacob, or Joseph, or Jesus—something like that—I forget his name, was heading toward town that day on his way south from Samaria. We knew that road well. It was about a mile from us, and it was relatively untraveled during the week. A group decided to go and at least get a look at this man. They invited me to go with them, but I didn't even have to think about it. No, I would not go, it would be a waste of time, I thought. But when they started to leave, I thought, *What else do I have to do?* So I caught up with them, and we found a spot along the road where we waited, and we waited, and we waited.

It was quite late in the afternoon when we saw a small group coming our direction. We moved off the road; (that was required by law when another person was coming). We watched. We kept our distance, but when he got alongside us, we couldn't keep quiet. We started to cry out, "Jesus, Master, have mercy on us. Jesus, can you help us? Have mercy on us." I don't know what we were expecting. I guess we were hoping for a small handout so we could buy some food. Maybe we weren't expecting anything. I just don't know.

But this rabbi stopped. He stood there and looked at us. Nobody had done that in a long time. They always looked the other way because we were truly the despicable of the earth in most people's eyes. He turned and said, "You have suffered long enough. Go show yourselves to the priest. By the time you get there, you will be healed." And with that he started to walk on.

We looked at each other in total skepticism. I know I felt stronger than I had felt in ten years, but not much else seemed to have changed. We set off through the field toward town to find the priest. It was only a little bit later, when we were halfway to town, that I looked at my hands and arms. My skin was clean. The rash was gone. I stopped and just stared. Then I had a dilemma. I had been raised to be polite; that was important in our family. We hadn't said "thank you" to the man. We hadn't actually said anything. What should I do? What if I went back to this rabbi and my leprosy came back because I didn't do what he had told me to do? What if I went to the priest and the rest of my body was still covered with scabs? I could go see the priest, and if I was actually accepted as healed, then I would try to find this Jesus and say thank you.

But that was not how I was taught. I told the other nine to go on ahead. I would catch up with them later, and I turned back toward the road. I walked as fast as I could, and I kept looking at my hands and arms to make sure nothing bad was happening.

When I got to Jesus, I stood off to the side away from the crowd (ten years of doing that instinctively made it a tough habit to break). But when I called out he saw me and motioned for me to come. He started coming toward me. I fell to my knees and said, "I don't know how you did it. I don't know why you did it, but I want to thank you. It's been ten years since I was whole. I will never forget what you just did for me. But tell me, I want to go home and show my parents first, but then what do I do? How can I be sure I never stop being grateful? You have given me back my life."

Jesus walked over and did something no one had done for years. He reached out, took my hand, and helped me up. Holding my hand, he quietly said, "You are well, but remember who you were. There are a lot of others who need your help. Don't turn your back on them. Do that and you will remember. Thank you for coming back. I bless you for that."

That was twenty years ago. I could still take you to the exact spot along the road where Jesus had taken my hand and helped me stand. I'll never forget that. I went to the priest, was certified as healed, and then went home to my family. On the way, I thought, *I have been blessed. I dare not forget the friends I have back at the leper colony. I am going to ask my parents to help. We are going to improve their living conditions, we'll make sure they get better food.*

I didn't think I could cure them as Jesus had cured me, but I could bring some comfort and human dignity to them. I knew that would help me never forget what Jesus had done for me.

—The leper's story is in Luke 17:11–19.

21. No One to Help Me

My life began in as normal a way as anyone could expect. I was a healthy baby, and for the first years of my life, all went well. Then, when I was about six years old, something swept through our village and many of the children began to get sick. Several of them died from this mysterious disease. I sometimes think they were the lucky ones. I did not get as sick as they did. I did not die, I only lost the use of my legs.

From that time on, my life was limited to as far as I could reach without having someone help me. My parents did everything they could, which in reality was almost nothing. There was no cure, and my legs never recovered. My parents had to provide everything for me. I was unable to work or move from place to place. I could, however, move my hands and arms, and my mind was clear, so I decided to teach myself to read. It was a slow process, but I learned to read, and I became a casual student of the Torah. Thus, my life, while severely limited, did have some creative expression.

After I became a man, or at least half a man, my parents began taking me to the pool at Bethzatha, near the sheep gate in Jerusalem. This was ever so much better than staying inside the house all day with nothing to do. Here were a number of other persons who were blind, lame, or paralyzed. Over the years we had formed a common bond. We would visit, there were others who could read, and we would talk together. Often people who came to the pool would give us alms, but virtually no one ever stopped to talk with us. It was as though they wanted to do their good deed and then get out of there as fast as they could.

Many people believed that the pool had healing qualities. At rare intervals, the pool would suddenly come alive—the water would somehow be stirred up, erupting into a boiling swirl. No one could predict when it would happen, and the story was widely known that on these rare occasions, the first person to get into the pool would be healed. There were some restrictions by the Jerusalem city government limiting how close we could be to the pool because others came to swim, and we dared not restrict their access.

I don't know what I believe about these healing stories. I never saw anyone actually be healed, but everyone was sure it worked, so we all stayed there hoping it might work for us. But when your legs don't work and there are twenty other people also wanting to be healed, I had no chance of ever being the first one into the pool. I needed the help of another person, but there was no one who would stay with me for weeks at a time in the slight chance that the pool would erupt. So years ago, I had stopped wasting my energy hoping to be healed. I knew it just was not going to happen.

Then one day, a man came through the pool area, saw me, and asked a strange question: "Do you want to be healed?" Why would anyone ask a lame man that kind of question? Of course I wanted to be healed! Doesn't every paralyzed person pray that they might be made whole again? And I told him that because I was paralyzed, I could never reach the water first, and other people always beat me into the pool. All I ever got for my efforts was to get soaking wet. I told the man that I'd stopped trying. It simply did not work for me.

Then he did something even more unexpected. He reached down, took my hand, and quietly said, "Get up. Pick up your blanket and walk." I looked at him, not knowing what to do. That was a ridiculous thing to tell a lame man. We just couldn't do that. But he gave my hand a gentle tug and nodded his head. "Come on. You can do it." I still don't know why I did it, but I pulled on his hand, managed to get my feet under me, and I stood up. I hadn't used my legs for nearly forty years, and it was something of a struggle, but with his help I got to my feet. I was wobbly, but I was standing!

The man let go of my hand, smiled at me and walked away. I didn't even get to thank him. I've always regretted that, but I was so shocked by what was happening that I wouldn't have had any idea what to say.

That's when the trouble started. I had picked up my blanket and was starting to walk around the pool to go home when some Pharisees stopped me and complained: "This is the Sabbath. You are not permitted to carry your blanket." That was interesting. I had read enough of the law to know that technically, you were not supposed to carry anything on the Sabbath, but I also knew there were exemptions that permitted it in my case since I was lame. Only I wasn't lame anymore, so I guess they thought the exemptions no longer applied to me.

I told them, "The man who healed me told me to do it, so I did. Now I'm going home." They stepped into my path and wanted to know who it was who had given me permission to break the Sabbath rules. I had to tell them that

that I had never seen the man before. He hadn't told me his name, he had just healed me and walked away.

That didn't make them any happier. They told me to put my blanket down. I could come back for it the next day, because I was required to obey the rules of the Sabbath. I told them I thought that was foolish. It was my blanket, I was going home, and I was taking it with me.

I left the pool and went toward home, going past the corner of the temple on my way out. That is when I saw the man who had healed me. He told me to use my new strength for the good of others. As he was talking, I heard another man call him "Jesus." I thought I would be polite, so I thanked him. Then I told the Pharisees his name was Jesus. I thought they would be glad to know that. If I had known how they would respond, I never would have told them. They got quite angry, and I heard them talking together about how they had to stop this man Jesus. I couldn't figure out why anyone would want to stop someone who was healing other people. Sometimes, the world just doesn't make much sense.

—The story of the paralytic is told in John 5:1–18.

22. I Don't Know Who I Am

I had no idea that life would be like this when I was a boy. I was an active lad in the local synagogue school, I learned the Torah, and I loved to play games with other boys. Life was good, and I assumed it would always be that way. Then one day when I was a teenager, it hit me. I was totally unprepared for it. I began to shake, and saliva ran out of my mouth. I tried to scream for help, but no words came, just sounds that had no meaning. The boys I was playing with got scared and ran away. I was terrified. I didn't know what was happening or what I should do. It lasted only a few minutes, but those few minutes radically changed my life.

Doctors couldn't find anything wrong with me. For days, I was watched carefully by my parents, who refused to let me go outside. Gradually, life began to return to normal. Some of my friends even let me join in their games. Then several weeks later, whatever it was hit me again. I was playing a simple game in the street when suddenly I fell down and began to shake all over. I could feel what was happening, but I couldn't speak. I made only nonsensical, babbling noises. By the time I started to calm down, all my friends had run away again, and this time they stayed away. Somebody dared to suggest that I had a demon, and that idea quickly spread through the town.

I didn't know what it was, but I was labeled "demon possessed," and there was no way I could defend myself. For the next ten years, I lived in modified seclusion with my parents. They did the best they could, but they didn't understand it either. Most of the time, I was normal, but every couple of weeks, I would lose control. I would scream and yell and say things I would never have said in my normal experience. I knew whatever it was would pass, and within a few minutes I would be normal again. But the problem was that there was never any warning. I never knew when the next episode would happen, and before I could prepare, it simply took over my body. Even I began to believe that some other force or power was taking control of my life. I couldn't believe it was me doing this.

The impact was devastating. I couldn't hold a job. I never finished synagogue school, something I dearly loved. Obviously I couldn't marry, and more and more of the time, I couldn't be part in any social gathering. I developed a reputation, and unfortunately, my behavior got worse and worse and became more frequent. That only served to validate the diagnosis of demonic possession. My parents tried hard, but when I was attacked by the demons, there was no way they could control me. Several times I tried to kill myself when I was being attacked.

The town even assigned military people to guard me. They chained me to the wall of an old building to keep me from hurting other people even though I had never hurt anyone during any of my attacks. It always seemed that these demons didn't like me because I would cut myself or throw myself down and cause myself a lot of pain, but never anyone else. It was a terrible life. I began to hate myself and this "force" that would take over my life.

I began spending most of my days out in the cemetery among the tombs because there I was alone and there wasn't too much I could do to hurt myself out there. I caused enormous pain for my parents because they couldn't help me no matter how hard they tried. So I had become used to being an outcast with everyone being afraid of me. I was convinced I was evil and possessed by the Devil. The best thing I could do was to keep myself isolated from all social company.

I had resigned myself to this terrible existence because it was the only thing I knew. But then one day a stranger came to our village. There was something different about him. Strange situations had a way of triggering my loss-of-control episodes, and I'm afraid that when I saw him, I lost control. He said something to me about not listening to the voices I kept hearing in my head, and I remember involuntarily falling down at the man's feet and shouting at him, "Oh God, let me alone."

He didn't flinch. He quietly asked me what my name was. I told him I didn't know who I was because I had been called lots of names. Something inside me begged him to let me go back to the life I had by then become familiar with. I didn't want to go away to a new place and have to start all over again. He said, "Those voices in your head don't belong to you. Don't listen to them anymore." He pointed to a huge herd of pigs that were stampeding toward the sea. He said, "There go the voices. They won't bother you again." And thankfully, they haven't.

He then took off his outer robe and gave it to me because I was standing there naked. The herdsmen for the pigs went to tell the owners what happened, and they pointed to the man as the one who had caused it. How they made that connection I don't know, but they were upset and demanded he leave before he caused any more trouble.

I sensed something had happened to me, but I wasn't sure what it was. I just knew that he had had something to do with it, and I didn't want him to leave. I begged him to let me come with him. I thought if the voices came back, at least he would be there to make them be quiet. But he said, "No. You stay here. Tell all your friends and neighbors what happened to you. Tell them God healed you, and let them see you are well again." And with that, he left.

I went back into town, got dressed, and explained to my folks what had happened. It was the first time I'd had made sense to them in years. My mother cried. My father was a bit skeptical but promised to wait and see.

Very gradually, I began to move back into public circles. After months had gone by and I had had no more outbursts, a few people began to talk with me. The circle just got bigger and bigger until almost everyone in town knew what that man had done. They didn't understand it, but they began to accept me, and I began to discover again what it meant to be a human being.

To tell you the truth, I didn't understand it either, and it took me a while to believe it really had happened. But it had, and I was very grateful to that man, whose name, I had learned, was Jesus. He never came back into our town, but I was certain that if he had come, he would have been warmly received and people would have listened to him. I know I would have.

—The story of the Gadarene demoniac is told in Mark 5:1–20.

23. Look Out Below!

My parents knew something was wrong when I was only a few months old. I didn't kick or move the way my older brothers and sisters had. I just lay there, alert and responsive, except I didn't move. That has been the story of my life. I can see what was going on around me, and I could understand everything people said about me. Why do "normal" people assume that people who can't walk can't hear either? People talked about me as though I were not there. Some would say, "What did he do wrong that he was born this way?" How could I have done anything wrong before I'd been born? They would say, "Why do you suppose God did this to him? I'm sure glad I'm not him. I wonder what it is like just lying there on that cot."

I could have told them what it was like, but nobody ever asked me. It was depressing and discouraging. There were many times when I wished I had not been born, or that I would die soon. Thirty years is a long time to be confined to a chair or a bed, and to know it would never get any better. My world was basically a small circle around my chair, only as far as I could reach. My parents did everything they could for me, but that was not much. One good thing was that they recognized I had a good mind. They arranged with the rabbi at the synagogue to bring me copies of the Torah, and with the help of my older brother, I learned to read. They also contacted some of their friends and encouraged them to talk about the Torah with me.

That was when I decided I could either be here and be miserable, making everyone around me miserable or I could accept that this is me, and make the most of it. I started showing interest in things other than myself. People began to treat me differently. Our neighbors would drop in for short visits and keep me informed about what was happening in the city. On nice days, my parents would put me in a chair outside the house. People began to talk to me rather than about me. I became a person who had a name. I was no longer just "the cripple" in Ezra's house.

That is when I first learned about a Jewish prophet/teacher named Jesus. I'd never seen him, but friends told me lots of stories about him. It seemed like the common people loved him but the religious leaders were not very happy with him. That convinced me that I liked him, because the religious people had never paid much attention to me. I had no money for the synagogue or the temple, so they treated me like I was of no value.

One day, four of my friends showed up. They told me Jesus was in the area, and they were going to take me to hear him. I told them I was not going to go, because there would be a crowd and I didn't do well in crowds. But they wouldn't listen. They made it clear I was going. They were going to pick me up and carry me whether I liked it or not. What was I supposed to do? I was in no condition to run away.

Just as I had expected, there was a big crowd at the house where they said Jesus was speaking. I told the men to take me back home. I could not see Jesus from my cot. I could barely hear anything he was saying. It was a useless trip, and I was tired. But they had put me down and were off a few steps looking at the house. There were the usual steps on the side leading to the flat roof. They came back and announced that Jesus was inside the house, so they were going to take me up the steps and lower me down through the thatch. They made it clear that I was to cooperate. As though I had any choice!

Well, that was more than I was prepared to accept, but just as I started to argue, I felt myself being lifted on my narrow cot. Then I was being taken up those outside steps toward the roof. Again, that was the story of my life. Other people told me what they were going to do to me, and then they did it whether I liked it or not.

I had never been on the roof of a house before. The view was beautiful over the city. While I was admiring my new surroundings, the men started opening a small hole in the thatched roof. They took some strips of cloth and literally tied me down so I wouldn't slide off the cot. Then they tipped me up and lowered me down through the hole. That was a new experience!

I was about halfway down when it got very quiet. I could see everyone looking up at me as I was being lowered down toward them. They moved back a little, and then I was on the floor, surrounded by people who didn't seem too happy to see me.

When Jesus saw what was happening, he looked up at my four friends on the roof and began to laugh. I remember he shook his head in amazement. I think it was a new experience for him too! He said, "Friend, your sins are forgiven." That was interesting, but it was not what I needed! I have never had much opportunity to be a terrible sinner.

That got some of the crowd upset, and they started to argue among themselves. They said he was not allowed to say that, but it seemed innocent enough to me. What Jesus probably knew was that a man in my situation was not able to commit many sins, so forgiving me was probably relatively easy. But the crowd was charging him with blasphemy!

I knew the law well enough to know that was a serious charge. They were arguing that only God could forgive sins, so if Jesus was forgiving my sins, he was claiming to be God, and that was totally unacceptable. When they got so loud and boisterous that Jesus heard what they were saying, he stood up and looked at them.

"What's wrong with you folks? Is forgiving someone's sins any harder than telling him to stand up and walk?" He turned to me with the slightest smile on his face. "Tell you what," he said. "Why don't you stand up and walk around so these narrow-minded people can learn something." He extended his hand to me. "Let me help," he said. I lay there for all of about five seconds and thought, *I'm going to do it.* I reached up, took his hand and got up. I was pretty shaky at first, because I hadn't done that for years. I took a look at Jesus, who was smiling. I think he was enjoying it as much as I was.

He gestured toward my bed, so I bent down, rolled up my blanket, and started to walk out right through the crowd. It was kind of funny as I think about it now. They were so busy arguing among themselves about whether Jesus was allowed to do that that nobody paid any attention to me. I didn't know if he was allowed to do it or not. I just knew what he had done, and I was thankful. I decided to let them worry about what the law said.

My four friends came bounding down from the roof where they had been watching through that hole in the roof. They slapped me on the back and offered to help. I told them I didn't think I needed it. If they would carry my blanket, that would help. I wanted to walk as far as I could before asking for help. If I felt I needed it, I would tell them. This walking stuff was new to me.

I was so grateful my friends insisted we go that day.

—The lame man's story is in Luke 5:17–26 and Mark 2:1–12.

24. Never Miss a Chance to Do Good

I was born with a physical condition that people who know these things would call a birth defect. My right hand never developed in a normal pattern, so I had some restrictions in what I could do, but as a boy, I learned to function quite well. There were limits to what I could carry, but I could read and write, and I could run with the best of my friends. My parents were really good about it. They guided what I did so I wouldn't get caught in impossible situations. My brothers were good about letting me play with their friends, at least most of the time, and they helped me with anything that called for two hands.

But several things were constant reminders of my limited abilities. I never thought a great deal about my restrictions until I began synagogue school. I could learn as easily as anyone else, and I always had my schoolwork done on time. But in that social setting, it was clear that most of the other students saw me as a second-class person with lesser abilities. Why would people assume that because I have only one hand, I must not be as smart as everybody else? Why do people make fun of persons like me as though we have no feelings? There were games I couldn't play, and I knew that. But I could do other things.

The religious restrictions the community placed on me, however, were really painful. I could go to the synagogue, but especially there, I sensed caution on the part of many people. They avoided physical contact as though if they touched me, my withered hand might cause their own hands to wither. No one ever said that out loud, but I could sense what people were thinking.

One day, one of the rabbis explained it to me. Our right hand is the normal, clean hand that we use for writing and eating and greeting friends. So if your left hand is inferior, that's not a problem. It has less value and is therefore unclean. It is an insult to greet a friend with your left hand. If my left hand had been withered, I would have been considered normal, but since it was my right hand, my whole body was less than normal and therefore unclean. Because I wrote and did virtually everything with my left hand, I was perpetually semi-unclean at best.

Did you ever think about why one hand would be considered cleaner than the other? Why should one hand control the whole body? When all the religious people, all the priests, and all the teachers kept me at arm's length, even when they did it politely, it was hard for me not to pick up the message that God was probably keeping away from me too.

It wasn't that I was openly rejected; it was more that I was never invited to be part of any group. It was hard knowing there was a party at someone's house but I hadn't been invited, even though all my "friends" were there. Or in synagogue, there are readings that are part of the regular service. All the other boys got chances to read these texts. I was never asked to be a reader even though I was one of the best readers in the class. When you are different from all the others, you notice these things even though no one else seems to catch on. Especially when I keep telling myself that I am NOT different, it is just that my right hand was shaped differently from theirs.

I had to learn to accept who I was and how to live with it. I had a job, and I kept going to synagogue even though it was a constant reminder of my lower level of acceptance. I learned to stay in the background, to not speak up, and generally act like I was not there even though I thoroughly enjoyed the regular readings and lessons.

There was one particular rabbi who occasionally taught at our synagogue, and I would never miss his lessons. He had insights that opened new understandings. He had a view of God that told you God cared about you when most of the rabbis left the impression that if you didn't do it right (there's that word again—right!), God was almost eager to punish you. But this rabbi would tell stories from our history about how God led us, forgave us, and urged us to do better. When he came to teach I always went home feeling better. Maybe God did know how I felt. Maybe I didn't have to hang around the edges. Maybe I could just be me, and that would be okay.

I was surprised one Sabbath evening after this rabbi finished speaking. He came down from the low platform and walked right over to where I was standing along the wall. He said he had seen me there quite often and wondered what my name was. Before answering, I took a quick look around because it had suddenly become very quiet. It seemed everyone was looking at us.

This rabbi—his name was Jesus—also realized everyone was quiet, but he said, "Let's go over here where we can see each other better." He motioned for me to come away from my dark corner out toward the middle of the synagogue.

He reached out and gently pulled my right hand out of my robe, where I had learned to keep it so people wouldn't see it. He held it in his hands—a new feeling for me. He turned to the crowd, looked the Pharisees right in the eye, and said, "Here is a teaching moment. Doesn't the law say we should do good things on the Sabbath, and not harmful things?" He looked all around the crowd, making a slow sweep with his eyes. He knew every one of them was looking at him, and I think he knew what they were thinking: *Don't do this on the Sabbath! Come back tomorrow and heal the man's hand. He can wait. It's not a life-or-death situation. Why can't you keep what the law says? Why voluntarily break the law like this? What are you trying to do to us?*

He turned back to me. By then, I was shaking all over. Was I going to get in trouble? I hadn't asked for this; I was a law-abiding Jewish citizen. What was going on here? All he said to me was, "Let's look at your hand. Show it to me." When I stretched it out, I saw it wasn't shriveled up. It was perfect! The skin was smooth, and my fingers were flexible. I could rotate it as normally as I could my left hand. I was amazed.

And then I heard it—the murmur of the crowd. It got louder. These religious people were complaining about Jesus because he had healed my hand. Nobody was paying any attention to me; no one said, "Good for you" or "Thank God!" or "Shalom." I felt like jumping up and down and singing, but everyone else seemed to be angry. Once again I was being pushed aside because somehow I was bad, just like I had always been treated.

As I think back about that day, I think Jesus was very deliberate in what he did. I think he knew the Pharisees would get angry because he didn't keep the law in exactly the same way they did. He took a more flexible, positive approach that said doing good was right even on the Sabbath. The Pharisees believed that doing anything on the Sabbath was wrong. Maybe they felt that way because they had never had withered hands or lame feet or anything else that would have kept them from being perfect.

I learned something that day that I have never forgotten. Doing good for others can be done at any time, and God will bless you for it. There is never a wrong time to do good. I think that was the point Jesus was making. Don't ever miss a chance to do good for other people, because that is a form of worship of God. Maybe doing good is more important than worshipping God at that moment!

—This man's story is in Luke 6:6–11.

25. Short Is Only in Your Mind

I never thought about being short. That is, not until my younger sister grew to be taller than me. Then I began to be teased by friends and playmates in Jericho. I hated that. Oh how I wanted to be tall like my friends! But that never happened. Throughout life, I was the shortest person in the group, and I never learned to accept that. My father told me that short was only in my mind. That became the driving force that turned me into an overachiever. I couldn't match my friends in physical height, but I was determined to pass them all in personal success.

I began to work with my father as I reached young adulthood. I was married to a fine Jewish woman, and we soon had two sons. One day, my father told me there was a tax collector position coming open the next month and they were looking for a Jewish person to take the post. He knew my aptitude with finances and thought it would be a good chance for me to go into business for myself.

That evening, I talked with my wife about the opportunity. It was an excellent chance that might never come again. I wanted to apply for it, but my wife wanted nothing to do with it. She felt it would affect our family life, and she wondered what it would do to me. I assured her it was a good opportunity, it would not change me, and if I didn't take it, someone else would. I felt that with my reputation for honesty, people would trust me and all would go well. She was not convinced, but she knew it was my decision.

One month later I started as a local tax collector. I began with the commitment to be open, honest and fair in everything I did. All went well for the first seven or eight years. Then the regional collector position became available. I knew with my experience that I could do the job, so I applied and was rewarded for my diligence.

Now I was supervising six other local tax collectors. My income was dependent upon what they collected so that I could pay Rome. I kept my old tax area, knowing it had the strongest potential for personal income.

I was making good money, but things were changing in my life. I discovered if I worked just a bit harder, I could increase my income substantially. I put a little more pressure on the tax collectors under my supervision, and my income increased. I began to think about finding a larger house so my children would have more room. They didn't seem to be as happy as they had once been. It was rare to have them invite any of their friends to our house, but they used to do that a lot.

Then one day, my wife and I talked about the house I wanted to buy and what our options were. We'd always talked about things. It was clear I was in charge, but I always listened to her counsel. This time, she was angry. The house we had was certainly large enough, especially since I was never in it. Had I noticed that the children didn't have any friends to play with? Yes, I was buying them lots of things, nice clothes—almost everything they wanted— but my work as a tax collector had built a wall between us and all our Jewish friends. How long had it been since I'd been to synagogue? I was not the father I had once been. My focus was on money, on things, on status with Rome. She wanted me to quit being hated by almost everyone. The children needed to have a father and friends, and my money couldn't buy that.

I didn't see what was wrong with what I was doing. I was certainly more honest than most of the other tax collectors. If I hadn't been doing the job, someone else would have been glad to have it, and then things would be much worse for us and our neighbors. I knew that some people didn't like what I did and avoided me in public, but any job had the potential to alienate others. I was sorry about the children, but they were much better off than any of their friends. I was in far too deep to quit now. There were a lot of people, mainly Romans, who were looking up to me, and I felt like I was important. I liked that feeling.

I was making my monthly collection rounds one day when I saw a crowd down the street. I had heard that there was a new rabbi in the community, so I decided to listen. It had been a long time since I had been to Synagogue. I was always busy, and besides I didn't feel welcome there, so maybe it would be good for me to hear this new teacher.

I soon discovered being short was once again a problem. The crowd was big, and I was on the outer edges. I couldn't see a thing. Just off to my left was a Sycamore tree with low hanging branches. I knew I could get up on them and I would be able to see without making a fuss. It wasn't hard to do. Now I could see and hear much better.

Jesus was walking toward me as he talked, and right when he was beneath my tree, he looked up and waved to me. "Zaccheus, come down. I would like to have lunch with you today." I was embarrassed to be identified that way, but I couldn't pass up this honor, so I jumped down and went over to him. Together, we headed to my house. I thought, "This was going to be good."

Our Jewish maid quickly set some food on the table while I visited with Jesus. He asked how I was doing, and I told him, "Very well, thank you." Then he asked how our children were, and I started to answer when I saw my wife frowning at me. Jesus interrupted, "they don't have many friends, do they? I see lots of things, but no friends. And your friends from synagogue, do you and your wife have friends there? What has happened to the Zaccheus who worked in his father's business? Are you aware of the price you are paying for what you are doing? Is this really who you want to be? Is being used by Rome really worth the loss of friends, of time with your children, of losing your relationship with your wife?"

How did he know all those things? But he went on, talking about self-respect, about being a vital member of the community, about how I felt every time I went into someone's shop to collect tax money (again!). What was it like knowing that people didn't want to see me, that they didn't want to be my friend?

We talked---well, mostly he talked, for over an hour, and he touched every spot in my life where I knew I was in trouble. He identified everything I hated about my job. He named people who used to be our friends. He ended with a couple of soft-spoken comments. "Zaccheus, you have gone down this road for a long time. Yes, it has made you rich, but you know you aren't happy. You don't really like what you do. You know you can do better. You could go back to having friends and to having time with your children and regain your self-respect in the process. Why don't you stop--right now? There are probably a few places where you need to make restitution. The Torah has guidelines for that. Get your life back. Be who you want to be, not what Rome is trying to make you be."

I had been looking at the floor for most of this, because I knew he was right. Then I looked up, and saw my wife. Tears were streaming down her face, but she looked more beautiful than I could ever remember. Something was happening inside me. There was something there that I had kept trapped for years, and it was longing to be free. I turned to Jesus, "will you come with me?" He got up, and we went outside. The crowd was still there, wanting to hear Jesus, but he simply said, "Zaccheus has something to tell you."

That day was a whole new beginning for me. The next morning, I began visiting people. I dreaded the first stop where I apologized, explained what I was doing, and returned the equivalent of one month's taxes. By the end of the day, I had a lot less money, and that new house was no longer an option, but I had people thank God right in front of me as I returned excess tax payments.

That evening, I told my wife, "I don't know how we are going to do it. I'm only half done, and we're going to run low on money. I don't know what will happen to us."

Her response was priceless. "I don't know either, but I know we can do it, and I know I have never been as proud of you as I am this evening."

The next year was hard, but we survived. We were much poorer than we had been in years. We started going to synagogue again, and people welcomed us. I went back to work with my father at half my former income as a tax collector. But the best thing was when I came home one afternoon and was met by my wife at the door. She was so excited. Three women had come to visit that afternoon, and they had asked her to join them the next day in a special synagogue project helping to put some clothing together for the poor. She looked so happy. She motioned for me to come inside, and I saw five children playing with our two boys.

Jesus was right. Salvation has come to our house.

—The story of Zaccheus is in Luke 19:1–10.

26. Just Doing Good

I knew from very early in my life that I was a special child. It was not simply that my parents told me that I was; I had experiences that were different. I kept them very much to myself because I didn't want to be different. I was not Jewish, although I grew up in a predominately Jewish culture and knew a good bit about the Jewish faith. I respected what they believed, but I would describe myself as a religious mystic with no particular religious affiliation.

I went to a traditional Roman school, and I had a special interest in the mystical arts. We studied the stars, the heavens, and the Greek gods, and I even became acquainted with the teachings of the Torah about Yahweh, the Jewish God. It was very interesting to see how the gods operated in the heavens and how people didn't pay much attention to such things. The Jewish people rejected that concept entirely, but I believed such knowledge of the heavens was helpful in understanding how people functioned.

Most of my time was spent being a teacher. I taught the normal classes in reading, language, and mathematics. My Roman school did permit me to teach one class in spiritual realities. As I was teaching, I often felt a new awareness of what was going on around me. I could sense the student who was not well when he came to school. I had learned that by applying pressure to certain parts of the body, I could alleviate pain and calm the mind of the students who were under special pressure.

Thus I was not really surprised when two of my students came to me and asked for help for their father. He was suffering from demon possession, or so they said. He was seeing things that were not there and hearing voices that no one else could hear.

I asked him to sit down and talk with me. I went over his head and neck, asking how it felt when I put pressure on various parts of his neck or head. When I squeezed hard just above his ears, he said he heard the voices.

I had him lie down. I applied pressure, really hard, on one side of his head and held it for a moment. He gave a convulsive shudder and then lay still. I took my hands away, and he said the voices were gone. Over the next few weeks, he had no more problems.

I thought that would be the end of it, but it wasn't. He told his friends, they told their friends, and people began coming to me for help. Some I couldn't help, and I told them so. But a few experienced dramatic changes.

I never charged anyone. Usually, it took only a few minutes, and it didn't seem right for me to make people pay for such a small service. I never thought of trying to merchandise what I did. When people came and asked, I did what I could. The folks seemed grateful, even those who didn't get much better. That gave me all the satisfaction I needed.

One day, three men showed up at my classroom near the end of the day. They were friendly enough when they asked who I was. They told me they had heard I was casting out demons and they wondered how I did it. I tried to answer them discreetly because I wasn't sure who they were or what they wanted.

I admitted that I had helped a few people but that was not what I did for a living. I told them I was a teacher. They wanted to know in whose name I was doing these demonic exorcisms. I replied that I was trained in the mystical arts but I was not part of any group. They wanted to know if I was a follower of Jesus. I said I'd heard his name but had never heard him speak. I had heard he was a preacher and prophet but I had no connection with him.

They told me I had to stop what I was doing because that was what Jesus did, and I was not authorized to do demonic exorcisms. If I wanted to keep on helping people, I had to join up with Jesus.

I was clear with them right away. I had no interest in doing that. I was simply trying to help people who came to see me, and they had no authority to make me stop.

With that, they left. I could tell they were not happy, but I never saw them again, so I continued helping people whenever I could. It just seemed like the right thing to do.

—This gifted man's story is in Luke 9:49–50.

27. A Cautious Faith

I have always thought that people are called with a certain mission in life. I knew my parents had very high expectations for me. We were a privileged family, and I was very grateful for the special opportunities I had had as a child. My parents were wealthy, and they believed that their success in business had been guided by the hand of God. They gave back generously to the community, were solid supporters of the temple, and were honestly admired by many people. My father had originally wanted to be a rabbi, but for reasons he never talked about, that didn't work out for him. He began a business instead. As his oldest son, it was inevitable that I would be encouraged to live out his dream. My parents sent me to a private school where I was tutored in Hebrew Law, and I become quite proficient in Greek language and culture.

Our national religious history was always my special interest. I wanted to know what our people had been through, how they had survived, and how these things had shaped their faith. This meant that even as a young man, I paid special attention to how our Scriptures were written and how they were to be read. I went from synagogue school to the School of Hillel, the most respected Jewish rabbi of our time. After four years with Hillel, I did a personal guided study of the relationship of God and the Torah.

But what was also important was that every time I came home, my father would want to know what I was learning. He would constantly remind me, "Don't forget where you came from. Don't let your education separate you from your people. You have a privileged life, so you must remember to speak for those who have not been as fortunate as you. Don't ever forget who you are." My father meant a great deal to me, and I made a commitment to keep in touch with the local people who were the lifeblood of the Jewish faith.

Upon completion of my studies, I was offered several teaching positions across the country. I chose to stay in Jerusalem, where I taught courses in Jewish Law and Interpretation, Theology of the Prophets, and the Life of Moses. I poured my life into teaching young, aspiring rabbis to be creative in how they read the Torah, compassionate in their application, and careful in their own spiritual lives.

I am happy to say that my teaching attracted excellent students. My classes in Law and Theology were always full. Students would come to Jerusalem just to study with me. My father's counsel helped me gain the reputation of being a committed man of faith and an exciting teacher who cared about people. The teachers in our school were quick to recognize this, and after ten years of teaching, I was elected dean of the Jerusalem School of Hebrew Faith and Life.

About the same time I was appointed to the National Council of Hebrew Faith, a group of teachers who were the official readers of the Law for the nation, offering specific counsel to the Sanhedrin in their legal deliberations. My father was very proud of me and my accomplishments, but he kept reminding me to stay in touch with the common people. "Make sure you know what the average man in town is thinking, and hear their questions," he'd tell me.

It was inevitable that I would hear about this young independent prophet (a man named Jesus) who was emerging as the leader of a small religious group outside Jerusalem. He had quite a following as a charismatic speaker with special spiritual gifts. It also seemed to me that he had a radical approach that was constantly challenging the system and calling for reform. I didn't pay much attention to him, because that was how I had been in my younger days—critical yet creative in my approach to the religious system.

Over the months, I would pick up the *Jerusalem News* to see whether there was any comment on what Jesus had said or done. I read these reports with real interest and would often chuckle to myself at the idealism of young people. They had good ideas, but fortunately, they grew up, became more realistic, and settled down. The next generation would have another one just like them, asking the same questions. One side of me liked what I heard and saw. We needed creative thinkers to help us keep our faith alive and vibrant. A faith that doesn't think is a faith that's not worth thinking about.

The more I read, the more interested I became. This prophet—if he actually was a prophet—had good ideas about God, about peace, and about how to apply the Law. He was saying the same things I had learned under Rabbi Hillel. I would have said some things differently, but he made sense. It is fine to talk about peace, because that is a central element in Jewish faith. But you have to be careful how you do it, because radical political groups on the edges of society would pick that up, and then Rome would get involved. That was never good for anyone. But I was determined to withhold judgment and give Jesus the freedom to say what he wanted to say. Generally, I approved in principle, because I was saying some of the same things in my own classes.

Then I saw it was reported that Jesus was going to be speaking in the city in a few days. I found where he was staying and arranged to have a very private, quiet conversation after the meeting was over. I was really looking forward to it, because this man was clearly an intelligent, informed person who believed what he was saying. I thought perhaps I could help him.

I will never forget that meeting. I was in his evening teaching session, and we talked for hours after it was over. We talked about the Law, about religious beliefs, about concern for the poor, about politics, and about the future of Israel. Jesus had the most polite, disarming way of taking my questions and turning them around. "I know that is what you teach, and I understand that, but what if you look at it this way? What if you take Isaiah's words and apply them this way to that question? How do you read what Moses said on that issue? We have to find creative ways to apply the law, or it becomes a burden to all of us." That comment brought me up short because I had said that a dozen times in my own classes.

I alternated from being pleasantly surprised at his questions to being a little upset by how he handled the Scriptures and then back to being amazed at the insights and connections he made. It was truly rare to find a young man who knew the Scriptures as well as he did. There were places where we disagreed, but he wasn't offended by that. His handling of Ezekiel's words about having a heart of flesh instead of a heart of stone—that gave a twist and a modern application that I'd never thought about. His ideas about how the things we believe should have an impact on how we live could have come directly out of my class on Application of the Law. When I asked him how the Law should be applied in our day, he had a truly brilliant understanding of it. I made a mental note to remember this man because I was sure he would make an excellent teacher someday. He had a brilliant future ahead of him. I was impressed.

It was over a year before we met again. It was during Passover, and just as the police had feared, Jesus was in town with quite a following, making a few public speeches. It happened that the Sanhedrin was meeting in full session, and a more-conservative member was arguing that Jesus should be arrested for disturbing the peace. He made his point and was urging the group to take a vote when I asked to speak. I quietly commented: "I would recommend that you read the Sanhedrin charter before you do anything that will violate it."

That surprised many in the group. I was accused of being a Jesus sympathizer and of not being in support of the temple. I responded, "Look. You all know me. I want the law to be obeyed as much as any of you. But you can't arrest someone for making speeches you don't like. You have to apply the law fairly, and we have no legal basis yet to take any action against this Jesus fellow."

They knew I was right, but I still heard them muttering, "Well, you know what kind of people come from his hometown."

Another year passed. Jesus continued to grow in popularity, and the government was getting more and more tense. A coalition of religious and political leaders had formed to figure out how to stop this man in case he had any ideas about running for religious office, because with the following he had, he might just get elected.

I was busy with my teaching responsibilities when they had Jesus arrested on some ridiculous charges and threw him in jail on an old, obscure, legal technicality. Then without notifying all of us, the Sanhedrin met, bribed a few witnesses, threatened the judge, and Jesus was executed before any of us could intervene. I was furious, and I told the Sanhedrin. I felt what we had done was unjustified, without merit, and blatantly illegal.

But it was over, and there was nothing we could do about it. I went to a good friend who lived in Arimathea and persuaded him to use his political connections to give Jesus a decent burial. Joseph wanted to know what I was doing. Was I a friend of this man? I told Joseph that it was a tragedy that this man had been executed. I know he said some stuff that we didn't always agree with, but you don't kill someone just for having a few ideas that threaten the security of the leadership. "I can't go to the governor," I said, "but you can. I will provide the things we need to prepare the body. You get us a temporary tomb for the weekend." We got the body off the cross and into a tomb before the Sabbath started. Otherwise, it would have hung there for two days in violation of our beliefs.

I still feel badly about not finding a way to stop the Sanhedrin even though I was not officially a member. What they did was wrong, and we should have stopped them. That was truly a sad day in our religious history.

—The story of Nicodemus is in John 3:1–21, 19:38–42.

28. How Was I to Know?

Why do people so quickly pass judgment on others who are different from themselves? Why do people think that because I can't see, I must not be able to hear either? I can hear very well, usually better than they can, so I hear their comments as they talk about what sin I'd committed that I was born the way I was am. What does sin have to do with being blind? I probably sin a lot less than they do!

I've never been able to see, so I had no idea what it was like to see. I had accepted the fact that this was how life was going to be for me. It was inconvenient, not because I couldn't see, but because of how people ignored me. My parents did all they could for me. I learned to get around the house and even navigate the streets between our house and the temple. I went to the temple regularly. I was not allowed inside to worship (the people there thought that God felt about me the same way they do—"Must be something sinful about him that we don't know about.") But I was allowed to sit outside the temple and beg for alms so I could live.

I was sitting in my normal place one day when I heard some men walking past. I could tell by the sound of their footsteps that they were men, and more than just two or three. One of them asked the standard question about who sinned. I was sick of that question, so I was really surprised by the answer another man gave. He told them that was a dumb question. "Let's use this situation to bring glory to God, not to condemn one who is struggling with life."

I heard him come over to me. He asked me to stand up, which I did. It was the same man. I recognized his voice. Then he put something cool and moist on my eyes and told me to wash in the pool of Siloam. I didn't know what to expect. But it was quite close by, and I had nothing else to do, so I went. I washed my face in the pool, and behold! I could see! I just stood there and looked around for a moment. I could now see all the things I had only felt or imagined before. The world is much more beautiful when you can actually see it. I could not believe what was happening to me.

I assumed that my friends would be as excited about this as I was. But they tried to put me back into that box of being a theological problem, only this time it was a different problem. People went from asking, "Why can't you see?" to asking, "Who did this to you?" Why couldn't they just be glad for me?

They wanted to know who had done it. How was I supposed to know who did it, I couldn't see who it was. I heard the name Jesus mentioned so I described what he did and what he told me to do. Then they wanted to know where he had gone. How was I supposed to know where he'd gone? I was busy washing my face! Why is it more important for some people to make an issue of everything instead of just being glad when something good happens?

That was bad enough, but then it got worse. I was being held responsible for what someone else had done for me. I didn't even ask to have anything done. Whoever it was had done something, I responded, and it worked. Why can't we just leave it at that and let me go home?

Then the Pharisees got involved and created yet another issue. They told me it was the Sabbath day. I already knew that. But they felt they had to know exactly what had happened in case this man had violated any Sabbath rules in helping me see again. So I told them again what had happened. Only this time I could actually see their reaction. They were nodding their heads. "This man is obviously a sinner because he does not keep our Sabbath rules." Then they had to talk that over among themselves. You see, they believed only God could heal, and since this Jesus, whoever he was, had restored my sight, he must be of God. But if he was of God, he would not have violated the Sabbath.

All these theological arguments seemed so stupid. I could see! You'd think they would have been glad about that. I guess their religious rules were more important than my life.

They finally got around to asking my opinion, not that they really cared about what I thought. I told them straight out that I thought he was a prophet. I knew that would set them off, but I was getting tired of their foolishness.

That was when they decided I was an imposter and not the person who used to be blind. So they tried to drag my parents into the discussion. My father would have none of it. He told them, "Yes, he is our son, and absolutely, he was born blind. But we were not there when all this happened, so how do you expect us to tell you what happened?" I thought that was a good answer.

By the way, I was delighted to see my parents for the first time. They looked pretty good, and they were thrilled beyond belief that I could see. They were as annoyed by the questions as I was. They told the Pharisees that I was an adult and I could speak for myself. Since I could now see, I guess they assumed that I could think, too !

So here we go again. They came after me one more time. They had made a decision, and I was to play along with it. They told me, "We know this man is a sinner. You should give glory to God because only God can do this. But you have to stop giving this Jesus guy any praise because we have decided he is a sinful person, so he cannot have done this."

By then, I was sick of their logic, and frankly I no longer cared whether he was a sinner or whether he was God. I just knew I could see, and that was enough for me. Let them argue the details. But that put them back at square one. "How did he do this to you?"

I'd had it with them and their questions. "I told you how it happened. Do you want to know who it was so you can become part of his group?" That made them angry. "You can follow him if you want to," they said, "but we follow Moses. We don't even know where this man comes from."

I thought, *What difference does it make where he comes from? I was blind, now I can see, and he did it for me. That's good enough for me. Your own logic does not hold up."* (You see, people who see often think people who can't see must be dumb. But not seeing has nothing to do with being smart or dumb!) I said to them, "This man healed me. You say only God can heal, so there must be a connection between this man and God!" I probably shouldn't have said that, but it is what made sense to me.

That made them even more angry, so they got personal and insulted me. "What gives you the right to lecture us, you stupid sinner!" And then they kicked me out of the temple, which was sort of funny because they had never allowed me into their temple in the first place.

Later that day, the man who had restored my sight found me and asked if I believed in the Son of Man. I asked who that was. I needed more information. He told me that he was the Son of Man and he had come to help people like me learn how to see. Finally, someone said something that made sense. I thanked him for what he had done.

But a couple of Pharisees heard what he had said and wondered if he was accusing them of not seeing things right. You know what Jesus said? "YES!" I couldn't help laughing to myself!

—The story of this blind man is in John 9:1–41.

29. A Matter of Life and Death

This has always been the way it was for me. In a culture where men were the identified persons, the ones who carried the family responsibility and who were the leaders in the community, it seemed I was always known as, "Oh yes, you mean the brother of Mary and Martha?"

It started that way when I was a child. I was born into a family that already had two daughters, one ten years older than me and the other fourteen years older. They were gifted sisters. They helped raise me, so I was always fighting an identity crisis. They were good sisters, but the three of us never really fit into the traditional Jewish model of the ideal family.

We were nontraditional in several ways. Mary and Martha exhibited strong leadership skills working in our parents' sewing and clothing repair business. They were leaders by nature, so they moved into the family business, which meant that there was no automatic place for me. I grew up as the little brother who had to be cared for and who was usually in the way.

It was a sign of our family's economic status that I was sent to a private school, where I developed a love for numbers. I later found my place as the bookkeeper for our family sewing business. That might explain why none of the three of us ever married. We were too busy, too independent, and too successful to have time for marriage. I'm certain that our commitment to working together in the family business was also a factor. If one of us would have pulled out to be married, that would have created hardship for the other two. So we remained our own family.

Mary, Martha and their brother Lazarus. People just couldn't figure us out. But we were comfortable together, we were secure financially, and we had many friends. It was through this network of friends that we first met Jesus. Neither I nor my sisters had much background in the Torah, so occasionally, we had friends over to talk about questions we had. We had invited several people over for an evening of thinking together about one of the synagogue lessons. We enjoyed these times together, and we were delighted when one of our friends brought a young rabbi to joining our discussion.

Have you had the experience of meeting someone and feeling as though you've known that person forever? We spent the evening talking about worship. Most of our group felt that worship was important but that it didn't always relate to what we were doing with our lives. This young rabbi was so stimulating. In his quiet way, he asked questions and got involved with us in thinking about how worship should help us be more aware of God's presence. This rabbi felt worship should intersect with our daily lives rather than call us away from it. I'd never heard anyone describe it quite as clearly as he did.

The evening ran later than usual, and we all agreed that we wanted to get together again. We urged the rabbi—Jesus was his name—to come stay with us whenever he was near Bethany. We had the extra space, and we wanted to keep this conversation going. Thus it was that Jesus became an almost regular guest in our home. Mostly it was for one night, but sometimes, it would be for two or three days. He told us that our home was comfortable, and he could rest so well in the quietness of our house when we were all at work.

There was some minor tension between my sisters. Martha wanted to be sure everything was clean and proper when Jesus came, while Mary felt that Jesus didn't come to inspect the house but to relax. If we were relaxed, it was much more likely that he could relax also. We were always delighted to have him with us.

We did face one particularly stressful evening. I'd been sick, and we weren't sure what it was. The rabbis couldn't explain it, and the medical people were sure it was just a passing thing. But when I was feeling so badly for nearly two weeks, Martha felt we ought to contact Jesus. I didn't want her to do that because I was confident I would be better soon.

But I didn't get better. Whatever I had dragged on and on, and at one point, I could no longer get out of bed. Martha insisted she was going to contact Jesus and ask him to help. I was too weak to object, and a message was sent asking Jesus to come.

That's the last thing I remember. I lost any sense of what was going on around me, except that I could sense Martha's anxiety when Jesus didn't come right away. I have no memory or recollection of what happened after that. It's all totally gone for me, I remember nothing.

The next thing I do remember is hearing Jesus calling me to get up. I tried, but I could barely move. I thought that they must have wrapped me tightly in something to protect me from getting an infection or to stabilize my temperature. I just knew my knees wouldn't bend, and it felt terribly awkward trying to walk toward where I heard the voice of Jesus coming from.

That was when people began to unwrap me. Thank goodness! I could barely breathe. The sunshine was so bright I had to blink and squint to see anything. A small group of friends were standing around, and Martha grabbed me, hugged me, and started crying. I still didn't understand what was going on. I couldn't figure out what they had done to me last evening while I was sleeping!

Then Mary explained to me that it was not last evening, it was four days ago, and I had died. They had done everything they could, but I had just drifted off into death. They had wrapped me for burial and had put me in the tomb. I was dead, and everyone was in shock and so sad. Then Jesus finally came and told me to get up. That part I remembered, but nothing else.

It was only later that Mary and Martha told me about what had happened, how Jesus did not get here before I died, and how upset they were. Martha explained how Mary was really angry with Jesus. She thought we were friends, but he hadn't come when we needed him. And look what happened!

Anyway, they told me that when Jesus arrived, they all came out to the tomb, where Jesus just stood there with tears running down his face for a few moments. He asked them to move the stone, and he called for me to come out, and I did! I have to take their word for it, because I don't remember any of it. I just know I am feeling much better and want to get on with my life.

One would think that everyone would want to celebrate with me and be glad that I was alive (if I really had been dead like they all told me I was!) But a couple of weeks later I discovered that the Jewish leaders were not at all happy about what Jesus had done for me. They were saying that my having my life back was a threat to the security of the nation. I even heard that there were some people who wanted to kill me. What! Make me dead again? I guess their reasoning was that my coming back to life gave Jesus too much publicity. I didn't see how killing me would solve that problem!

People asked me, "What was it like to be dead?" I don't really know. I guess it is because I was dead and wasn't thinking about what it felt like. I know that when I came back to life, it was as though I had just awakened from a really deep sleep. Those four days are still a total blank to me, like it was a long period of uninterrupted sleep. I would like to be helpful, but I can't describe something I have no recollection of. I am just glad I am here –alive-- and not there -- dead!

I think I can also say that I am not afraid to die anymore because it was not a terrible experience the first time. If you ask me, I would say that Yahweh was with me in that experience just like Yahweh is with me right now in this experience. I don't always consciously feel that presence, but I know it is there.

It took a long time, but gradually, life returned to normal. People stopped looking at me in funny ways; they stopped asking strange questions. They even started asking if I am still keeping the books at our family business. That tells me life is really back to normal again.

What do I tell people about my experience? Enjoy your life, live with enthusiasm and gratitude because we never know when we might stop living. Make your life count for something. Be glad to be alive. I know I am.

—The story of Lazarus is in John 11:1–44 and 12:8–11.

30. Take a Deep Breath

I was born into a fine Jewish family. My father was a rabbi, as was his father before him. At an early age, I learned to love the Law. I knew I wanted to be a rabbi in the synagogue. The Law made sense to me, and I wanted to be a teacher. My parents were delighted. They supported my work all the way through synagogue school and private rabbinic training in Jerusalem. Upon completion, I was given an assignment as rabbi in my hometown. Now that I had a job, I was able to marry. Soon My wife and I had a daughter who immediately became the love of our life. For some ten years, I couldn't imagine my life being any better.

So it was with some interest that I learned about a prophet/teacher who was going around the area talking about the Law. Since that is my life's work—I had studied the Law intensely for nearly six years—I knew what the Law said. I didn't agree with this young, untrained preacher when he was critical of how I and my rabbi colleagues were teaching the Law. I knew that the Law was the way to create a fair society and the best way to guide people into righteous living. It was also the best way to help the poor.

This young preacher had the nerve to tell us how we should treat our enemies. Well, I had responsibilities in the synagogue to protect our nation from the enemies who were all around us. I knew, and I taught, that the Law calls us to be practical with life. I also knew that you cannot change the Law. We have to trust God that careful obedience of the Law will entice God to help us in our times of need. So when members of my synagogue asked, I told them not to listen to this radical young preacher. His message was not the solution for Israel's future.

I stayed firm in my opinion even when people asked me about the supposed miracles that were reported to have been done by Jesus. I reminded people that there had been many other times in our history when the prophets had done miraculous things. The fact that this man was doing them didn't mean he was of God. Remember in Egypt, when God did miraculous things through Moses, the Egyptian religious leaders in Pharaoh's court did exactly the same thing—turning their staffs into serpents and such. I continue to be amazed at the shallow thinking of ordinary people. We who were teachers in the synagogue had to stand firm in our faithful reading and teaching of the Torah. We'd had challenges like that before, and I assumed we would survive this one too.

One evening, my wife met me at the door and said that Sophia, our nine-year-old, was sick. She didn't know what it was. She assumed it would pass quickly, but she wanted me to be prepared to call the doctor if she didn't get better.

Three days later, she wasn't better, and her strength was failing. The doctor had been here twice and had given us some medication, but he wasn't very positive because he was not sure exactly what it was.

You can understand what happened when five days later, my wife sent a messenger to the synagogue telling me that Sophia was much worse and that I should come home right away. My wife immediately insisted that I send for the young prophet Jesus and ask him to come help. I refused because I did not see this man as a man of God. He was a charismatic person who was able to sway crowds with good speeches, but that did not make him a man of God. I called for the doctor.

My wife continued to argue with me. "He can't make it worse, and maybe he can help. This is our daughter! How can you not do everything possible to save her life? How can you do this to her—to us?"

By the time the doctor got there, Sophia clearly was not doing well. I was devastated. Sophia was our only child. My wife was distraught, and she would not give up. "You must get Jesus."

What would you do? Your child is dying, your wife is furious with you, and the trust you tell others to have in God is not helping you at all. One last time, my wife confronted me and simply said, "GO!" So I went.

I found Jesus in a discussion with his disciples. I took a deep breath, went up to him, and asked if I could have a word with him. He nodded, and we walked ten or fifteen feet away. I turned, went down on my knees, and quietly pleaded, "My daughter is near death. She is my only child. Will you please come? Isn't there something you can do?"

He nodded and indicated he would come with me. We had only gone a short distance when there was a commotion caused by a woman who had pushed her way through the crowd and began talking to Jesus. I could hardly believe it! My daughter was dying, and this woman believed she had the right to stop Jesus. Fortunately, she took only a moment, and we moved on. But that delay cost my daughter her life. One of my servants came to tell me that Sophia had just died. Jesus heard the message. He quietly said to me, "let's go quickly."

When we reached our house, musicians from the synagogue had come to provide appropriate, Torah-prescribed music, and other members were there to share in our grief. Jesus did not approve. He told them to stop their funeral music because it would not be needed here. He asked all the people to go outside, while he went in where our daughter was lying. He paused, said a short, very quiet prayer, then reached out, took Sophia's hand, and pulled her up. I gasped and stared. My wife shoved past me, grabbed Sophia, and hugged her with tears streaming down her face. She turned to Jesus and uttered an emotional "Thank You! Thank You!" I nodded my thanks because I could not find words. What was going on here? I was seeing it, but I could not explain it.

How do you argue with evidence that is right before your eyes? I didn't know what to think of Jesus. How could I be critical of one who has just restored your own daughter to life?

As Jesus was leaving, I caught up with him before he went outside and said to him, "Sir, I am very grateful for what you did for me, my wife, and my daughter. I don't know what to think. Can we meet together and talk sometime soon? I have questions." Jesus gave me the slightest smile as he nodded his agreement. "Your daughter will be fine. Just give thanks to God." And he was gone.

We never did have an opportunity to have that time together. But when people asked me, I gave an honest answer. I would not consider myself a follower of Jesus, but I can no longer be critical of him. Our theology says that only God can heal, that all healing is from God. And for that I will always be thankful.

—The story of Jairus is in Mark 5:22–24, 35–43, and Luke 8:40–56.

31. Tell My Brother

I had an older brother who always let me know that he was the older one and that I had to do what he said. He was the boss because he knew more, and that is just how it was. I had better learn to live with it. That was okay when our brotherly fights were over minor things, but as we got older, he continued to take the same approach with everything.

Then a crisis hit our family. Our father died unexpectedly, and we were suddenly faced with the responsibility of dividing the family property. This was a critical responsibility, even though the inheritance was relatively small.

My brother was married and had four children. I also was married, and we had two children. But that was understandable because my brother had married five years before I had. It is only right to assume that in another five years we would have two more children, matching his four. Then there was the issue of who would inherit the house and who would take responsibility of caring for Mother.

It just happened that I have been fortunate in that I have a good job, with a good employer, while my brother has a slightly lower-paying job. That should not reflect badly on either of us because we have different interests and different skills. But my slightly higher financial income has allowed me to have a slightly larger house---not much larger, but we do have an extra room.

My brother argues that since I have a higher income, he should receive a higher percentage of the family inheritance because that would bring us closer to being equal in what we have. He felt that was fair. I told him that our individual incomes have nothing to do with dividing the inheritance.

So he went to the rabbi, explained his situation and his point of view about how the inheritance should be divided. Knowing my brother, I don't doubt he told the truth. I just don't think he told *all* the truth. My brother told me that the rabbi thought his point of view was appropriate and that this would be the fairest way to do things.

My brother and I have always been good brothers. We actually liked each other, but when he tried to cheat me out of my share of the inheritance, I got angry. We have not spoken to each other since that meeting with the rabbi.

I have always been a religious person. Actually, we both are. I had been to hear Jesus teach on several occasions. I liked what he said. He seemed wise and fair in his thinking. Yesterday, Jesus was in town, so I went to hear him. After he was done speaking, I went up to him and said, "Teacher, tell my brother not to cheat me in how we divide the family inheritance." I knew I would get a wise response from him, one that I could live with.

But what Jesus said was not what I was expecting. He avoided a direct answer by asking who had told me that he would be a judge in matters like this? And then he went on to make a big deal of it.

"Right here," he said, "is a prime example of what happens to a family relationship when you are greedy." I resented that because I am not greedy. I just want my brother to be fair with me.

But Jesus went on. "Life is ever so much more than the things you own. If you keep wanting to have more, you will never have enough, and you will lose friends in the process. If you spend your time accumulating more and more, you will wear yourself out and die not being content with what you have."

Jesus went on to say a lot more, but I didn't hear it very well. I thought I would get some help from him, but he didn't seem to be very sympathetic to my situation. He kept talking about life being more important than just the things we have and how much better it would be if we worked on building relationships rather than having more possessions. I went home, not knowing what I was going to do. I certainly hadn't gotten much satisfaction from Jesus.

That evening, my brother came over and said he wanted to talk. He started by saying he didn't like it that we weren't speaking to each other. That had never happened to us before. He said it didn't feel good and that it was upsetting Mother.

Then he really surprised me. He told me he had been to hear Jesus that afternoon (I never saw him there—I hope he didn't see me!) He told me Jesus said relationships were more important than the things we owned.

He went on, "I got to thinking the family inheritance is not that big, and it certainly is not enough for us to fight over it. Could we work it out this way?" He laid out a new option that neither of us had thought about before. We would each take an equal share of the inheritance and give mother the same equal share. If she could live with me, because we have the extra room, he would contribute toward her food and other costs. If either of us found that burdensome, we pledged we would talk together so that our relationship would stay strong. He was determined that money should never come between us as a family.

Wow! I remembered hearing Jesus say things like that, but it hadn't registered with me as it had with my brother. I felt a little ashamed of myself. I quickly told my brother how good his idea was and that I would be glad to live with it. I told him I would be glad to provide the room for mother if we could share the food costs three ways, with the two of us and mother contributing. That meant he wouldn't have to pay quite as much each month.

He liked that. We had an agreement, but even more important, we were brothers again.

—The story of the two brothers is in Luke 12:13–21.

32. My Mommy Taught Me to Share

It was summer, and my friends and I loved it, because that meant we could play together most of the day. These were exciting times in our country. The constant presence of Roman soldiers was a daily reminder of Roman control, but they never bothered us when we were playing. Our family was poor, but then, everyone we knew was poor, so we were just like everybody else. I heard my parents several times talking about a young teacher who was going from town to town talking about hope for a new world and better times ahead for the poor. My parents were interested in that, and I knew the parents of my friends were also listening to the stories about this man Jesus. He must have been pretty important because everyone seemed to know about him.

One evening, Father and Mother sent my brother and sister and me off to bed early. They told us to sleep well because the next day we were going on a picnic. We were leaving early in the morning to go hear this teacher Jesus. They told us, "We think he's going to be down by the sea, and this is probably as close as he will ever be, so we decided to do that tomorrow. We will take a picnic lunch and make a day of it. It will mean about a five-mile walk in the morning, and we want you to be strong."

That was really exciting news. I was ten and didn't care too much about hearing a teacher talk about the Law. But if we were going, I was pretty sure some of my friends would also be going, and that meant we would have fun.

The next morning, we started out early, but even then, we were almost too late. We were not the only ones on the road. There were dozens of people, and it seemed like with every step we took, more people joined us. Before we got to the sea, there were thousands of people, more than I had ever seen in my whole life.

By early afternoon, we were all sitting down on the hillside overlooking the sea, and the teacher began to talk. I wasn't much interested, so my father said I could go with some of my friends and play, but I should be careful not to get lost. We played for a couple of hours and came back to where our parents were still sitting. The teacher was just ending, and I asked mother if I could have something to eat. She shook her head. "Wait a few minutes."

Then I saw some men wandering around, asking if anyone had any food they could share. I looked at mother because I knew we had brought a small picnic lunch, but she just shook her head no and put her finger to her lips indicating I should keep quiet.

I watched for a few minutes. I guess no one had any food. That seemed strange to me, because I knew all my friends had brought their lunches with them. No one went away from home for a day without taking food for lunch. I sat down beside mother and whispered, "Mother, they must want some food for Jesus, because he has been talking for a couple of hours. I could give him some of mine. I'll get by without lunch. I'm not really hungry."

Mother responded, "Nathan, we brought a little bit, but it is just enough for us. Let those who have more than we do share theirs."

"But mother," I said, "you always taught us we should share, and if he is hungry, I think we ought to share. Why can't I give him my lunch? I promise I won't eat anything. I want to do it. He may need it."

I jumped to my feet before she could stop me, snatched my little satchel, and ran off to catch one of the men. When I got to him, I told him I had some cookies and a couple small pieces of fish that Jesus could have if he was hungry. I told him I was strong and didn't need it. (That wasn't quite true because I was getting hungry, but it was too late now.) The man thanked me, took the bag, told me I was a very fine young man to share like this, and went off toward the teacher.

I went back and sat down between Mother and Father. Mother put her arm around me and gave me a big hug and whispered that she was very proud of me. Father just patted me on the shoulder and nodded his approval.

Then the strangest thing happened. The men with Jesus started back through the crowd asking people if they needed something to eat. Almost everybody shook their heads no and pulled out their own lunches they'd had with them all the time. I was not surprised at that because that is what everyone did. You took a little food with you until you got back home. But what surprised me was why didn't anyone else say that they had their lunch. One single lunch would never feed this huge crowd, but if almost everybody had a small lunch with them, we would have had plenty for everybody.

The people sitting around us got out their own lunches, and we started passing bits of bread back and forth. They shared with us, and we shared with each other, and we all had plenty to eat. I had a lot more to eat that afternoon than I would have had if I had kept my own lunch and eaten it!

I thought about that on the way home, and I asked my father what he thought. I will remember his answer. "Most of us are afraid to share because we don't trust other people to share with us. What you did this afternoon was really important because you taught all of us to share with each other. That was a good lesson. I hope you will remember that when you get older."

I am much older now, but I still remember that day. I don't know why I felt so strongly that I should share my lunch. Maybe it was because my mother taught me I should share!

—The story of this boy is in Matthew 14:13–21, Mark 6:32–44, Luke 9:10–17, and John 6:1–14.

33. The Questions of a Young Boy

I've lived my whole life around the temple. I was born into a priestly family, and for as long as I can remember, I lived under the umbrella of the law. That was good, because I knew the law was given by God for our instruction to help us understand how we should live as God's chosen people. It was never a burden for me because I knew that it showed how much God cared about every aspect of my life. It is reassuring to believe in a God who has that kind of direct interest in all that I did.

My parents enrolled me in synagogue school, where I learned to read Hebrew and some Greek. Our Scriptures had just been translated into Greek because that was fast becoming the common language of the people. It was also essential that we knew Hebrew to read the ancient texts as they had originally been written.

As we studied the law, we also learned a lot about our religious history and the difficulties we had had when other nations controlled our religious and political life. I learned how Moses had led our people out of slavery in Egypt and the ways God worked through him for our deliverance. I learned about the years spent in exile in Babylon, where Ezekiel brought together the ancient texts into one collection so we would have a record of our history and our religious writings.

As I studied these texts, I thought a lot about our own immediate history. Living under Roman law and Greek culture complicated our faith, because Rome demanded certain things that came very close to violating our sacred texts. I learned the importance of keeping God central in our lives while trying to survive the control of a pagan government. I found these studies to be both exciting and discouraging. It was exciting to see how God raised up leaders to protect us and our faith, but it was discouraging to see how frequently people were willing to compromise the basic principles of the law to avoid standing up to Rome.

Following synagogue school, I was fortunate to be accepted into the School of Shammai, one of the best teachers of our time. This put me with a group of twenty other students, all of whom were included because of their excellent work in synagogue school. We were to be the next generation of rabbis and priests. It was an exciting challenge.

For four years I studied with Shammai. He was an excellent teacher, demanding that we know the law but also how to interpret and apply the law faithfully to contemporary situations. He taught us that the law was sacred and was not to be compromised. If we compromised the law, we were putting the life of the nation at risk.

Our study methods were challenging. We would be paired up in teams, and we would create situations that seemingly had no easy solutions. Then we would fire questions at each other as we searched for the right answer that would preserve the law yet be fair in the judgments we made. This became my life—asking questions and searching for answers. Shammai would not accept easy answers. He would point out a detail we had missed, and we would have to go back to work with our questions and answers.

When I had finished my studies with Shammai, I was given the post of assistant rabbi in one of the local synagogues. My work was not nearly as exciting as my studies had been. I was assigned to teach young boys how to read Hebrew and to guide them in memorizing sections of the Torah. Teaching young boys was frustrating because they didn't want to ask questions; they simply wanted to learn the right answers. I tried hard to instill a curiosity in them, but it was unusual to find any student who had the time to think about what questions to ask. But I worked hard at my task, and I was a good teacher.

When I turned forty, after about eighteen years of teaching Hebrew, I was offered the position of rabbi in the temple in Jerusalem. That was quite an honor, and I accepted it gladly. Now I was no longer teaching Hebrew. I got to supervise the younger rabbis who did the actual teaching. My work was given over to careful study of the law and mediating conflicts that arose in how the law was interpreted. Once again, life became exciting as I was constantly given difficult problems to solve and was giving serious counsel to other leaders

Nearly a thousand years earlier, King David had set up a rotating system where each month, a different set of rabbis would come to Jerusalem and actually do the work of offering sacrifices and conducting temple worship. This was an excellent program because it was like giving rural rabbis a special seminar in the Torah and worship of God. I loved the more serious interaction with these rabbis. They seldom had the chance to engage in serious Torah studies, so they were eager to learn.

We were just coming through the exciting festival of Passover. People came from all over the nation, wanting the experience of temple worship for themselves and their sons. The crowds were generally huge, their enthusiasm was obvious, and while it meant long days, it was always a good experience.

One year, it was the second day of Passover, and four or five of us were together in the temple. We were reviewing some of the topics and texts that had come up in that day's festival celebrations. We noticed a young boy, maybe thirteen or so, sitting a few feet away, all by himself, quietly listening to our discussion. We thought nothing of it, for men would often come in and sit around the edges for a short time as we discussed the law.

But this young boy stayed. And the next day he was back again, just quietly listening and thinking. When he came back the third day, I asked his name and where he was from. He told us his name was Jesus and that he lived with his parents in Nazareth.

Our group was smaller that day because most people were starting for home, so I asked the young lad if he would like to come sit closer. I said that if he had any questions, he should ask them. I told him that it would be okay, that we would be glad to talk with him. He seemed pleased to be invited. He came into our circle and listened for about an hour before he said anything. Then he wondered if he could ask a question. We didn't know what to expect, but we assured him to go ahead.

We were pleasantly surprised by the questions he asked. "When Moses gave the law, how did this change what we had believed when we were in Egypt?" His second question was even more perceptive. "What do we do if we face a situation that the law does not speak to? Where do we turn for help?"

For several hours, he asked questions and we discussed them together. He also made a few comments on how the law was being taught in the synagogue. He was always polite and respectful, but it was clear he had been really thinking about these things. Some of his questions showed exceptional thought. For example, "The law originally said we should love our neighbors. Why have people added to that saying that loving our neighbor does not mean loving our enemies too? Aren't we really all human beings before God? What do we do when the law we are being taught is slightly different from the law as it was written?"

That one got us thinking. I didn't know that anyone had asked that question before. We all knew that we had the responsibility to apply the law, but I had never been challenged to think about what authority I had to suggest alternative applications.

Just then, a middle-aged couple came around the corner of the temple, shrieked a shout of joy, and came running to the boy as though he had been lost. I had wondered about his parents, but he seemed quite at home with us, and he certainly was safe with us in the temple.

But his parents were surprised to find him with us. The mother was a bit perturbed and scolded him for not having stayed with them. She said they had been looking for him for three days. I wondered about that. Three days? They must have been frantic. With the questions he was asking, why hadn't they thought of the temple as the first place to look? Were they not aware of the excellent intelligence and insight that this young boy had?

As they were leaving, I told the parents how proud they should be of their son and what a good job they had done in teaching him the law. I said that he would make a good rabbi and that I would be glad to include him in my class when he finished synagogue school. With that, they left.

My temple staff and I sat for a while thinking about the questions this lad had asked. It was really unusual for a young boy of his age to wonder about such matters. I remember telling my staff that undoubtedly we would hear from this young boy again. People with his intelligence and curiosity were exceedingly rare. We would be fortunate to have more young men like him.

—The story of the priests meeting with Jesus in the temple is in Luke 2:41–52.

34. Helping People Worship

I come from a very religious family who was always active in support of the temple. From very early in my life, I loved going to the temple and seeing the magnificent columns, watching the smoke from the sacrifices float up to the sky, and hearing the beautiful music by the men's choir singing the Psalms. Worship in the temple was a wonderful experience.

My parents worked for the Jerusalem Bank. Their assignment was to operate a booth on the street just outside the temple walls. The temple treasury could accept only Jewish coins as offerings to God. Roman or other national coins were considered unclean and thus unacceptable. In order to make it convenient for worshippers who came from other countries, the bank was there to change money into local coinage so it could be accepted as an offering. I worked with my parents, and when they got older, I took over managing this sacred service we provided for worshippers.

It was an important task that required a good bit of skill and knowledge. We had to know what all the various Egyptian, Roman, Babylonian, and Greek coins were worth in order to make a fair exchange. Plus, we had to determine the commission rate for each transaction.

What really made it hard was that other merchants were setting up stalls right beside our official bank location. These merchants sold doves, pigeons, sheep, and even cattle for sacrifices as part of temple worship. You can imagine what kind of racket and smell that created. Then there were other merchants selling religious trinkets that worshippers could take home as memorabilia of their experience in Jerusalem. I did not like that. Worship should not be a touristy thing used to make money.

So one day, a group of us who handled the financial exchanges went to the temple officials and asked, because of the hectic confusion outside on the street, if we, and only we, could move inside to the outer court of the Gentiles and set up our bank exchange booths in a more peaceful setting. We promised to stay off to the side and not interrupt the Gentiles or the women who used that area for their worship. We felt our presence would not be disruptive in any way.

The temple leaders agreed that this would make worship simpler for the men who came to offer sacrifices, so they agreed with the stipulation that we would set up our stands along the wall and only along the wall. That was a simple thing to do, and the problem was solved.

That is, until the trinket merchants also wanted to distance themselves from the cattle and sheep dealers. They also appealed, and even though we bankers objected, they were given permission to move inside the temple proper. Only this time, there was not enough open wall space, so they were required only to stay "close to the temple walls." That was awful, because they, unlike us, were actually invading the worship space designated for Gentiles and women.

And then, like a ball rolling down a hill, the dove and pigeon merchants felt they were being discriminated against, and they wanted inside "for the convenience of their customers in worship." I was furious, but they also got permission. I told my other banking friends, "Just you watch. In a year, the cattle and sheep will be in here too." I was wrong. In six months the cattle and sheep were inside the temple walls. It was absolute chaos. We had successfully moved the chaos from outside to where it was now chaos inside. It was crowded, noisy, and smelly. The outer court was no longer a place of worship. It had become a marketplace.

From my vantage point near one of the gates, I could see what was going on, and during festival time, it was an absolutely crooked racket. I had wondered where all these lambs were coming from that were offered as sacrifices. Then I saw how it worked. Families would bring their own lambs as sacrifices only to have the inspection priests—of course in collaboration with the official lamb merchants—find a blemish in the animals and have them rejected. The merchant then offered to sell them a spotless lamb so they could have a family sacrifice.

The merchants then offered to take their lambs since it would be dreadfully inconvenient for the family to have to look after their lambs for the three days of festival celebration. That was not so bad until I saw the merchant put the lamb into exactly the same pen from which he had taken the "perfect" lamb that he had just sold to the family.

Sure enough, the next day, they did exactly the same thing, rejecting other lambs that had been brought in, then presenting yesterday's "imperfect" lambs as today's "perfect" lambs ready for sacrifice.

That made me very angry, and after work that evening, I went to the temple priests and protested what I felt was an immoral practice. The priest assured me that I must be mistaken, that would never happen in the temple, and besides, the lamb trade was not part of my responsibility at the temple. The priests would look into it when they had time. I should stick to exchanging money. If I continued to make trouble, they might have to move my own stall outside.

I could not believe what I was hearing. I had a very good business going, and I was not going to risk losing it, so I kept quiet, but I was boiling mad.

It was only two days later when late in the afternoon a young man came in and just walked around, looking at all that was going on. At first, I thought he might be a temple inspector—maybe they were checking on the lamb merchants after all. He stopped at my stall and politely asked a few questions. "How long have you had your stall inside the temple? Hadn't the bank been outside on the street?" I responded, "Yes, but this is more convenient for the worshippers."

"Where do the women and Gentiles worship?" he asked.

"I don't know, but it is so convenient for the men."

"But this is not what the temple is for. You people should not be here," he said.

"But we have the full support of the temple management, they want to make worship as simple as possible," I told him.

With that, he turned and left.

The next morning, I spotted him right away. We had just started our day, and he came through the open door (he was not walking—he was striding--with purpose). He grabbed a cage of pigeons and hurled it against the wall. He picked up some rope and began lashing at the cattle until they stampeded. That created total chaos. Then he walked straight over to my table, looked me right in the eye, and kicked the legs out of the table so that my money—my whole day's banking supply—went all over the place. He kept looking at me and said, "You know better than this. This is a place of worship, and you have made it a marketplace. God is not pleased, this must stop. Get out of here!"

Why had he picked on me? I was one of the good guys, an honest banker just doing his job to help strangers worship God. What was his problem anyway?

He systematically moved around the room, upsetting tables, opening the gates of the sheep pens, and setting doves free. The place looked like God had sent a mighty wind of massive proportion. For sure, no one could worship in this mess. He paused on the way out, turned and shouted, "This is God's House! Get out of here! The prophet Hosea was right. God wants mercy and justice, not sacrifices." And he was gone. What kind of crazy, radical fanatic was he? Of course people could worship here, and I was only trying to help. He was causing all the trouble.

I was down on my knees trying to find all my money. I think I got most of it, but I know this was not a good day in the temple.

—The story of Jesus in the temple is in John 2:13–22 and Mark 11:15–19.

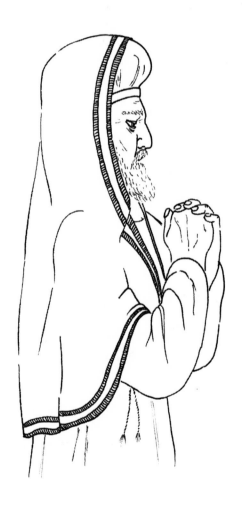

35. What is She Doing Here ?"

I have always been a religious person. When I was a child, I went to synagogue school, and the rabbis there quickly saw I had potential, so they recommended that I continue my study of the Torah at the School of Hillel, the leading rabbi in the Pharisee tradition in Jerusalem. All my life I have been immersed in the Torah and what it means for us as Jewish people to have been chosen by God over all the other peoples of the world.

Upon completion of rabbinic school, I returned to my home village and served for ten years as teacher in the synagogue there. I was well received, and I worked hard as a teacher of the Law. I was invited to move to a larger town and join the team of rabbis at a large synagogue. I was deeply involved in the community. I loved the dialogue time with the three other rabbis of the synagogue, and enjoyed being a leader both in the synagogue and in local town matters.

I had married a devoted Pharisee woman, we had two children, and life was very good to us. We enjoyed a comfortable home, so that we could entertain members from the synagogue for meals. This kept us in close touch with the people of the community.

I had heard about Jesus and had even gone to hear him teach. Most of what he said was quite stimulating. He had a prophetic tone in his message that got rather sharp at times, but then our prophets Amos and Micah had done the same thing. I was disappointed, however, with the criticism that he leveled at religious leaders and institutions. I suppose there are things that we could have done better, but we were called to teach and obey the Law, and that is an awesome challenge. I have always prided myself in knowing the letter and the spirit of the Law. I have kept the letter of the Law in great detail. I have always believed that one should not be teaching the Law if one was not obeying it in your own life.

I sent a message to Jesus, inviting him to come to my house for a meal. I wanted to talk with him, hear more about what he believed, hoping that I could persuade him to soften his tone and speak in a more positive way about the good things the synagogue was doing. I was looking forward to stimulating conversation about God, the Law, and the future of our people.

I knew that he was from Nazareth, a small town that didn't have the cultural advantages enjoyed by Jerusalem, so I decided to have a lighter, more informal lunch on our outside patio. I felt he might not be comfortable in my house, which reflected the status I had as lead rabbi at the synagogue.

We had just gathered around the low table and had barely started our conversation when a woman opened the back gate and walked up to where Jesus was sitting. She stammered something about being grateful for what Jesus had said a couple of days earlier, and then she burst into tears. She fell at his feet and pulled out a rather expensive jar of perfumed ointment. That is when I saw who she was. Jars like those identified her as a "woman of the street." My wife would never have allowed such a jar in our house.

I was amazed that Jesus accepted what she was doing without hesitation. That said a lot about him, because no legitimate rabbi would have allowed her to get that close, much less uncover his feet and wash them. That told me, this Jesus was not a legitimate prophet of God!

I stood up to call for my servants to remove this woman from the premises. That's when Jesus looked at me and said rather quietly, "Simon, there is something I want to say." I had the feeling it would be best if I not add to the confusion of the moment, so I nodded, assuming Jesus would find a polite way to distance himself from the woman.

But instead, he attacked me, telling a story about debtors that I had even used in my teaching at the synagogue, so I knew where he was going with it. But instead of criticizing her, he turned on me, and criticized me for being so informal with him. And I had done it for his benefit, to make him feel at home!

I actually agreed with the point he made about people who have sinned a lot need a lot of forgiveness, but everyone in town would agree that I was the model of a sinless life. The distance between me and this woman was absolutely enormous. At this point in her life, she did not deserve forgiveness. She was continuing her sinful ways. If she would only stop her sinful ways, repent of what she was doing, submit to the laws of the synagogue, and prove it by living a righteous life free of sin, then we could talk about forgiveness.

I am not used to being talked to the way Jesus came at me. I pride myself in being a good, moral person. I teach the Law, lead in offering sacrifices, and model righteousness in how I live. I was being blindsided by Jesus, and I did not appreciate it.

But Jesus did not apologize one bit for what he did to me. Quite the opposite; he turned to this woman and told her she was forgiven. That is something I never would have done. Just think of what that would have done to the morality of our community. I can see it in the *Jerusalem Post*: "Local rabbi hosts prostitute for dinner and forgives her!" Not in my house! How could I explain that to my colleagues at the synagogue?

—The story of Simon the Pharisee and the woman is in Luke 7:36–50 and John 12:1–8.

36. I Was One of the Good Guys

Sometimes, you need to know a person's family history before you really know that person. If you had known my grandparents, you would have a good image of who I am and where I come from.

My family ancestry comes out of Nabataea, a country a short distance south of Judea. They had moved there over one hundred years ago to escape the harsh rule of Antiochus IV, who tried to destroy the Jewish faith in Palestine. Those were hard times, especially for those who took their faith seriously. Many Jewish families moved to Nabataea, where they could retain their Jewish identity without risking persecution by Syrian soldiers. My grandmother married a very fine Arab man who had become a God fearer, one who retained his national culture, while accepting Jewish religious faith.

We lived in a mixed culture near Petra, so their marriage was easily accepted. I was the second of three sons. My two brothers have Jewish names, but Mother wanted one of her sons to be named after her grandfather, so I became Malchus. My parents assumed that Nabataea would be our permanent home, so my name was quite appropriate.

Several times, our family made the trip to Jerusalem for Passover. Those trips made a big impression on me. The excitement of the trip, the beauty of the temple, and the spiritual impact of the rituals led by the priests appealed to me. On our second trip, when I was about fifteen or sixteen, I told my father about my interest in becoming a priest.

I knew money was a problem, so I suggested that we explore the possibility of my going as a servant in the high priest's official house for several years. That would give me a better understanding of what it means to be a priest. So my father contacted our rabbi, who contacted the high priest and explained who I was, what I wanted to do, and what I had to offer as a servant to the high priest. The rabbi told me my chances were slim, but we should have hope.

Two months later, I received a reply from a servant of the high priest indicating that there was an opening for a servant who would be available to the high priest to deliver messages, run errands, and accompany the high priest when he traveled. They told me it was a menial job but that I could do some studying along with my work. I was ecstatic about working with the high priest, and to study at the same time was perfect.

One month later, I was in Jerusalem, where I started my work as a student of the Torah and servant to Caiaphas, the high priest. That was six years ago, and I have been an eager student. I have been learning on the job as I have also been learning in the synagogue about the Law and the prophets of Israel. The prophets have been especially exciting for me. Their vision of what faith should be, their challenges to the religious system when it strayed from its original purposes, and the concern they had for social justice were important factors in shaping my own faith.

This was exciting, but I was beginning to be aware of conflict within myself as I studied what the prophets were saying and compared it to some of the things I saw in the daily temple practices. I wondered what the prophets might say to us if they were here.

Don't get me wrong, I loved my work. My studies were challenging, and I had high respect for the high priest. But there were times when I longed for a modern prophet to speak out on behalf of the poor and to challenge the expensive practice of sacrifices in the temple. We needed a new Amos, or Isaiah, or Ezekiel.

I wasn't helped by what I was hearing about a rebel prophet from Nazareth. We had talked about John the Baptist in my studies, and most of us saw him as a legitimate critical prophet who had something important to say. But then, when this Jesus followed John, we saw the potential for a movement that would challenge both temple worship and Torah observances.

Have you ever been pulled three ways at the same time? Those were difficult days for me. Caiaphas was very critical of this new prophet, claiming he was endangering the life of the nation and could easily cause major trouble for the temple if Rome ever heard what he was saying. My teachers and colleagues in the synagogue classes were also rather critical, but they considered him to be a fresh voice that we should listen to. I went to hear Jesus several times. I know I was young and idealistic, but every time I heard him, I felt within myself that this is what we all needed.

I kept all this to myself because I didn't want to lose my position as personal servant to the high priest, nor did I want to jeopardize my studies. But I knew inside myself that Jesus was saying the kinds of things I felt needed to be said. I never actually met him, but I had a feeling that we would meet someday.

It was the week before Passover when I was given a series of special tasks. I knew there was a lot of anger in the high priest's office about Jesus; they wanted current information on what Jesus was doing, where he was going, and what he was saying. So I was told to follow him and report directly to Caiaphas every day on his schedule. I could tell something was going on, but I had no idea what it was.

I was in the temple watching Jesus when he made a mess of the place. When I reported this to Caiaphas, he was absolutely furious because he had a lot invested in the temple and all that went on there. I had also learned that Jesus and a small group of followers would be observing Passover in the home of Mary, a place where they often met. I had also heard that in the past several years, after the Passover meal, the group had gone to Gethsemane for a time of prayer. When I reported this to Caiaphas, he rather impatiently said, "Yes, I already knew that would be happening." I wondered how he had come to know that. Who else was watching Jesus?

That led to a very interesting assignment on Thursday night of Passover. I was told that I should go with a group to Gethsemane and prepare a very thorough report of all that happened. I was not told what to expect. I was to be careful, pay close attention, and report everything.

So that evening, I met the group as scheduled. That was my first shock. These were not high-priest types of people. I knew no one except a man named Judas, whom I had seen with Jesus on several occasions. Most of the group looked pretty tough, and I suspected some might even be zealots, which made me uncomfortable. But even worse, there were three Roman soldiers. What were they doing here? I wasn't sure I wanted to be part of this group. Some of them were carrying swords, but my task for the night was just to watch and report, so I went with them. But I was still confused about what was going on.

This group of about twenty got to Gethsemane, and Judas, who seemed to be in charge, led us back into a quiet, wooded corner, where we found Jesus with a couple of his friends. That was as close as I had ever been to Jesus, so I edged my way in to see as much as I could. I heard a short exchange between Judas and Jesus, and then Jesus asked the crowd who they were looking for.

With that, a couple of men in the group lunged for Jesus and grabbed him. Then one of the friends of Jesus pulled a sword and took a massive swing. I saw that sword coming at me, and I instinctively ducked. But I wasn't fast enough. That sword hit the side of my head. I felt a stabbing pain, and I felt blood running down my face. My hand went to my head. My ear was missing! Then it hit me. That guy with the sword thought I was part of this group that was trying to arrest Jesus, and he tried to kill me. I thought Jesus believed in peace. Who was that guy, and why had he picked on me? I am one of the good guys. Why would anybody want to kill me?

That is when I got weak in the knees and started to collapse. Things got blurry, and I must have been losing consciousness. But I do remember Jesus quickly coming over and kneeling beside me. He took his robe and wiped the blood from my face, and he put his hand on my ear—the one that wasn't there anymore. Somehow, the pain stopped, and when I felt it, my ear was back in place. I heard Jesus quietly say, "I am sorry this happened. You will be okay now."

The soldiers grabbed him and took him down the hill toward town. I just lay there for a few moments until I felt strong enough to walk. I went right to Caiaphas and gave him a full report. He ignored completely everything I said about my ear. All he wanted to know was, "You are sure the soldiers arrested him?" I said yes, and he immediately left in a hurry to go someplace.

I have thought about that night quite often—about how close I came to being killed and how Jesus healed my ear. It still hurts a little bit once in a while if I bump it, but I can hear very well.

I don't know for sure what I am going to do about Jesus, but I think I will stop working for the high priest. As I put the pieces together in my mind, I think he had something to do with what happened that night, and that is not what I think religion should be doing.

I wonder if anyone will pick up on the things Jesus was teaching. I hope they do, and if they do, I think I want to be part of that group.

—The reference to Malchus is in John 18:1–11.

37. I Only Wanted to Help

The first time I heard Jesus, I knew he was the one. I had grown up in the small town of Kerioth, far to the south of Jerusalem. Life was hard in Kerioth. We had suffered at the hands of the Romans several times, and as a young man, I saw up close and personal what Rome did to innocent people who dared to oppose their abusive policies. My father, Simon, was a supporter of the Zealot movement, believing that the only way the Romans would leave was if they were driven out. The only hope we had of that happening was with guerrilla warfare.

In my childhood, I remember my father being gone for a day or two, and when I asked where he was and what he had done, I never got a straight answer. He was always gone "on business." But we were farmers, and I didn't understand what kind of business would take my father away from our flocks and fields. What I do remember is that my father often talked about how terrible the Roman occupation forces were and how we dared never lose the hope of freedom from Rome.

I was with my father in Hebron one day. We had gone there to sell wool in the marketplace. Late in the afternoon, Father wanted to leave to hear a man teaching about the hope of Israel. I wondered about it because we had not yet sold all our wool, but I went with him. We heard a prophet make strong claims about how he was the promised one from God and how we needed to join with him to drive out the Romans and establish the kingdom of David in a new way.

On our way home that evening, my father told me that this prophet was the best hope Israel had ever had. I saw excitement in my father, and he explained to me how the Messiah would come like a new King David and how he believed this prophet would make that happen.

Tragically, a few weeks later, we heard that this prophet had rallied a small army and had attacked the local Roman military base near Hebron. It was a disaster. Nearly one hundred Jewish men were massacred by Rome, including the prophet. Our family was devastated. What we had hoped for was not going to happen. Life would continue on under Roman domination.

That was when I was just a young man. About twenty years later, my father had died. I was working as an accountant for a small business. I was in Jerusalem where I heard a young prophet named Jesus, from Nazareth. He was talking about the kingdom of God, and I paid close attention. I listened for about an hour, and I knew I wanted to be part of this movement. I talked with him afterward, explained who I was. I told him that with my background, I could be very useful to his movement as an accountant and treasurer. I explained to him how my father had taught me about the kingdom of God and how I was prepared to work hard to make that happen.

Jesus said that he was forming a team and invited me to be part of it. I immediately said yes, and I became a loyal follower of Jesus. He had vision. He knew how to read the Scriptures, he could teach, he was charismatic with people, and I saw how quickly he inspired people with his message. With my organizational skills, we would work well together.

That was the beginning of a very exciting three years. I listened to Jesus talk about laying down our lives for others and about moving away from our past. I got frustrated with the other disciples because they would argue among themselves about who would get what positions of power in this new kingdom. They simply didn't have the passionate zeal I had. I would not have given them any positions of authority.

I was very pleased with the way Jesus reached out to the poor. That was going to be the base for our whole movement. We could count on them because they didn't have much to lose. When we gained control, they knew we would take care of them.

But there were times when I got frustrated with Jesus. He missed good opportunities to recruit people who would have been very helpful when our time of action came. And he was not very good with money. Often, he healed people and never asked them to pay for it even though they had plenty of money.

One time, he really made me angry, and I spoke up. A woman had come with a very expensive bottle of perfumed lotion and wasted it washing Jesus' feet. If she had given that bottle to me, I would have sold it and used that money to buy things for the poor so that we could be sure of their support when we started the revolution.

That is when I decided it would be wise for me to set aside a regular portion of the money people gave us so we would have the resources to buy the equipment we would need to get our new kingdom started. I didn't tell the other disciples because they would not have understood. I had to stretch the truth a couple of times when they wanted to know exactly how some of the money they thought we had had been spent. But I knew it was for a good investment, and I didn't use any of it for my own personal benefit.

Everything was going exactly as I had expected until we got into the middle of the third year. Maybe it was just my imagination, but I detected a slight change in Jesus' attitude and approach. He became a bit less forceful in his preaching. He even began talking about how God wanted us to love our enemies and how we shouldn't resist people who had power over us. That did not fit very well into what I knew about King David's model for the kingdom of God that Jesus had been talking about.

I remember clearly the day when Jesus asked Peter what people were saying about us. Jesus got rather irritated with Peter when he tried to steer Jesus back on the right path toward how this kingdom would achieve leadership power. Jesus had been talking about how some of us might even die. That got me all excited, because I fully expected that some of us would die in battle with the Romans. If it was for the kingdom of God, I was prepared to die.

But over the weeks, it became increasingly clear to me that the edge was gone in the vision Jesus had for a new kingdom. He had lost the intensity and passion of his vision to remove Rome. It was so obvious in that stunt he pulled riding a donkey into Jerusalem two days before Passover. That sent exactly the wrong message. If I had known what he was going to do, I could have arranged for a couple of horses and put together hundreds of people. We could have really challenged the power of Rome with a display of people power that would have given our movement a tremendous boost.

It was halfway through that pathetic display of weakness that I knew what I had to do. Someone had to get Jesus back on track, and with Passover just a few days away, this was exactly the right time to do it. If I could just set the right things in motion, I could put Jesus in a position where he would be forced to use his power to defend himself. I had heard him talking about wanting to have an evening in Gethsemane, and that would fit perfectly. If I could get a couple of soldiers out there along with some zealots, we could stage his arrest, and Jesus would have to act. We could kill a few soldiers, and that would start the revolution. Everything would fall into place, and history would remember this as the greatest revolution ever.

The real genius of it was that I could use this as a fundraiser for the revolution. I would tell the high priest where Jesus was going to be, and for thirty pieces of silver, I would lead them to him. It was perfect. We make some money, some soldiers get killed, Rome responds with force, and Jesus would call for those seventy-two thousand angels he once told us were just waiting to help. That would give us a power base that Rome could not ever match. All I needed to do was get Jesus back on track for the revolution that would change the history of Israel. There is no way it could fail.

The next day, I got to work. It only took a couple of hours. The high priest almost eagerly gave me the money. Maybe I should have asked for more! They also arranged for the soldiers, and I supplied a small crowd of armed zealots. This was going to be good.

I really don't know what happened. Everything was right on schedule. I left the supper early and was waiting in Gethsemane when Jesus and the disciples came. My zealots came after it got dark. I had to calm them down when they saw how easy it would have been to have killed the soldiers right there. I told them to wait. They would have their chance to do that after Jesus had been arrested. My plan was working.

But then Jesus messed it all up. I identified Jesus as promised with a loyalty kiss. Then Peter, that impulsive guy, pulled a sword and attacked an innocent servant of the high priest. That changed the whole thing. Jesus stepped forward and almost voluntarily allowed himself to be arrested. That was not how it was supposed to happen! Nobody got killed, and the revolution fizzled out right before my eyes.

As I watched Jesus quietly being led off by the guards, what I had done hit me hard. Instead of starting a revolution to save Israel, I had set Jesus up to be killed. I had effectively ruined all hope of God's new kingdom ever happening. I was responsible for the death of the one person who might have saved Israel. How could I have been so wrong? I tried to stop this right then!

I ran back to the temple and told the high priest the deal was off. I threw their money at them, but they just laughed at me. I had ruined all hope of Israel's liberation from Rome.

I wanted to die!

—The Judas story is told in Matthew 10:4, 26:14–16, 27:3–6, and John 6:66–71.

38. This Is Not How I Had Planned It!

As I look back, I tell myself I didn't really have a chance. My parents lived in poverty. They tried to raise me right, but we never had enough food. I never had a real bed to sleep in at night. Most of what I wore I had stolen from shops, from travelers, even from friends. We scrounged for food in Hades, the Jerusalem city trash heap. We lived off what other people threw away.

As a young man, my life was dismal. I had no time for friends, there was very little work, and Roman soldiers were everywhere. It was quite by accident that I met Jesus. I had no work that day and was out on the streets hoping something good would happen to me. Little did I know the good things that were about to happen for me.

I saw a man who was talking to anyone who would listen. I had nothing better to do, so I edged closer. He was talking about a new way of living, a way in which the poor would be cared for, the hungry would be fed, and people would not be constantly suffering under Roman oppression of our political and religious environment.

This man was talking a language I could understand, not like the rabbis in the synagogue. I had stopped going long ago because what they said had virtually no connection to my life or my future. But this man talked about poverty, hunger, and suffering. Those were all things I knew about through personal experience.

I heard Jesus teaching on the street several times in the next week, and I kept wanting to hear more. If there was a better way, I wanted to know about it. By the end of the month, I was an enthusiastic supporter of what he was saying. I never officially joined up because no one was doing that, but along with a group of others, we all knew we were looking to this Jesus for leadership.

For the next few months, I worked whenever I could, but when there was no work, and that was often, I was out listening to and trying to help Jesus. He was the one best equipped to make life different for people like me. He was telling the rich to share with the poor and those who had plenty to eat to help those who were hungry. I liked his thinking, and I wanted to be part of his group when this began to happen. I hoped it would be soon.

I was with Jesus two days in a row one week, and it was really troubling. On the first day, I heard him talking about how all of us should share with others, about how we should stop wasting energy by hating Rome and its soldiers, about how we should take charge of our own lives in following God. He even told us that God's way was the way of peace. That got me thinking. What good is peace going to do for us? Rome would just drive us further into poverty if we ever gave in to their demands.

The next day, it got even worse. Jesus talked about loving our enemies. I had no intention of loving any Romans. I wanted them out of the country, and I thought Jesus did too. I didn't know that loving Rome was part of the bargain. I just did not agree with Jesus about that.

The next day, it got still worse. Jesus was telling stories about our ancestors suffering in the wilderness, and about how we should have a radical new way of thinking, that looking out only for ourselves was not the way God wanted us to be. He was urging us to put the good of others ahead of our own desires; that way, all of us will be better off. I didn't see how that would work. I knew from experience that if you didn't look out for yourself, others would abuse you and beat you up. You had to take care of yourself because no one else would do that for you.

It was at that point that I, along with some others, finally said no. Jesus was not making sense. Following him would only mean more misery. I did not see how I would get much out of it for myself. So I walked away. It had been good for a while, but he was simply asking too much with this loving the Romans idea. You have to take care of yourself if you want to get ahead in life.

There was no work for me, so I went to Jerusalem with some friends. The city certainly had something to offer. One day, I saw a wealthy man carelessly put down his money purse while he was buying some fruit. It was so easy. I simply grabbed his purse and ran. I was out of sight before he knew anything had happened. I had more money than I had ever had in my life.

Two days later, I was back in the marketplace. This time, I went around to the back of a stall, and when the merchant was talking with a customer, I reached into his bag and took a handful of coins. He would not know it until evening, and then it would be much too late. This was easier than working.

It was inevitable that once in a while I would get caught by either the Jewish police or a Roman soldier. I would spend a couple of days in prison, but then I'd be back out again. I used my time in prison to build a network of friends. We weren't really friends, but we learned from each other how to avoid getting caught, who the easiest targets were, and how to get in and out of Roman properties more quickly. I never intended to be a thief; it was only a temporary thing until I could find a job. I worked alone. I was angry most of the time, and I had lost all contact with my parents years ago.

Living on the streets like I did, you see life from the bottom up. Survival becomes the primary goal, and gradually, I slipped into a pattern of crime that slowly escalated in intensity and violence. I will never forget the first time I killed a man. He was a nobody, a common thief much like me, but he tried to steal some of my things that belonged to me. Actually they didn't belong to me technically because I had stolen them, but I had possession of them, so I guess they were mine. I caught him one night rummaging through my sack while he thought I was sleeping. He should have known better. He died because he was dumb.

That is how life was for me for the next year. I was good at what I did, and I was doing well on the streets. Passover season was coming, and that was always good for my line of work. Visitors from out of town were not that careful with their money and I could make in two or three days what normally took me a month to make.

I still don't know how it happened. It was late one night; I had just relieved a Jewish merchant of a sizeable purse when he grabbed my arm and started yelling for help. I could not get free so I hit him, hard. He fell, hitting his head on the street. I could tell instantly he was dead. I started to run—right into the arms of two Roman soldiers. What were they doing out that time of night? I had forgotten about Passover. There were always a lot more soldiers around during Passover. I had done the one thing I vowed I would never do. I had been careless.

I was thrown in jail for killing a Jewish merchant. The next day, I was tried and convicted of murder. Rome didn't take much time for these things. I was sentenced to be crucified in two days.

There is no such thing as an appeal of a Roman sentence. Two days later, I was dragged outside the city, unceremoniously nailed on a cross, and was left hanging there until I died. It was me and two other guys. That's when I saw him. The third man I didn't know, but in the middle was Jesus, the teacher I had thought was going to save people like me. How did he end up here? What did he do?

The other man started heaping all kinds of abuse on Jesus, telling him to act like God and get us down. I had the time to think about how my life might have been if I hadn't walked away from Jesus just over a year ago. I never intended to die like a common thief. I didn't know what Jesus had done, but I was sure it was not anything that warranted crucifixion. I finally told the other guy to shut up. We were guilty and we knew it. This man was not guilty of anything more than helping people dream about how life could be. Then I turned to Jesus and the last thing I remember saying was, "Jesus, do you remember me? I once followed you because I thought you were the Messiah, but I walked away. I should have stayed with you. I would not be here if I had stayed. Can you forgive me for turning my back on you? Will you put in a good word for me with your God?"

I remember Jesus telling me, "Yes, I promise you will be with me, and I will be with you."

Dying on a cross is excruciatingly painful, but I felt a strange sense of peace as I endured a couple more hours, and then I died, believing my future existence would be an improvement over this life.

—The story of the thief on the cross is in John 6:66 and Luke 23:32, 39–43.

39. Speaking Out—Too Late

I came from a very traditional Jewish family. We faithfully attended religious festivals and weekly synagogue teachings and obeyed the instructions of the Torah. My parents recognized very early on that I had special gifts and an interest in religious matters. That pleased them very much, and they encouraged me to enroll in advanced studies in the School of Hillel. Along with these religious studies, I did special studies in business and management because I knew some day my father would expect me to take over the family business.

My studies with Hillel had a significant impact on me. He was a more open rabbi and believed that God was more interested in the welfare of people than in their rigid obedience of the law. He taught that the law should serve humanity, not the other way around. That became one of the central beliefs that stayed with me all my life. The law was given to help people. I had seen that in how my father conducted business, and as a result, we were quite successful.

I first became a partner with my father. Then when his health began to fail, I took over the company with a commitment to continue the policies and practices he had begun. Things went very well for me. I had married, and we two sons and a daughter. I was glad when they also showed interest in religious studies. We often sat around the table discussing points of the law as it related to business issues, with caring for the poor, with proper Sabbath observance, and whatever else seemed to be important.

Our table discussions became a bit more intense when my two sons expressed appreciation for a more radical preacher who was making quite a stir about the need for renewal in our daily practices of Jewish faith. I didn't pay much attention, because this man was radical, and I was comfortable with my own faith as it was. But you know how the younger generation is. My sons were enthusiastic about this John the Baptist preacher. But then sadly, John said a few things that made the Roman governor angry. John was arrested and then executed. He was not the first to feel the heavy hand of Rome, and he probably would not be the last either.

Within a few months, another voice began to be heard across the countryside. My sons said this was a relative of John the Baptist, and he was picking up the themes John had emphasized. He was from Nazareth, a small town of no great importance. But according to my boys, he was a voice for the future and would need to be reckoned with.

Well, a man in my position as an active synagogue supporter, a member of the council, and a prosperous businessman, had to be careful about the people with whom our family associated, and I warned my boys to be careful. But one day, they asked if they could bring this Jesus to our house. They thought I would want to meet him. We arranged to meet at a quiet eating place several blocks from my home. That seemed safer to me because it would call less attention to what I was doing.

I was immediately impressed. This Jesus had a lot of the same ideas that I had learned from Hillel. He stressed human relationships and put less emphasis on the technical, legalistic requirements of the law. He talked about helping the poor. (I was already active in supporting the food distribution programs in Jerusalem.) He spoke positively about the dignity of women. (My wife and my daughters were always included at the table when my boys and I talked about the Torah.) He told us we should do all we could to reach out to others with understanding. (I believed in being flexible with my clients.)

It became immediately clear that Jesus and I had a lot of the same ideas, but I was not sure how it would look if we were seen together too often. Already I had heard comments by other Sanhedrin members about how this man was dangerous and could get us into trouble with Rome. I didn't see that at all, but it was best for me to keep quiet about what I thought.

Over the next two years, Jesus and I met together whenever he was in our area. We never met at our house, but I always found quiet, out-of-the-way places where no one knew either of us. I knew my sons frequently went to hear Jesus speak at public gatherings. That was all right because they had their own lives to live. They knew I approved of Jesus and that I often gave him money to help with his ministry. Sometimes, they argued with me about why I did not just come out and be public about my support for him. Why not tell people that Jesus was right and that I believed he was doing a good thing? They argued very logically that I was an influential religious person in the Jewish community and we even had the respect of the local Roman officials. Why not use that influence in a positive way for Jesus?

These were good questions. I guess I am just more cautious and careful because I have a lot to lose if anything went wrong. Jesus knew I supported him. He also knew I would never say anything against him, although I probably could have said some positive things on several occasions when people raised questions about who this man was and what he was doing. I was comfortable staying in the shadows. It was better for business that way.

The week of Passover was a dangerous time. I watched from the side as more-radical Jewish men were attacking Jesus, challenging what he was saying, and twisting some of his statements to make them sound really bad. I knew what Jesus believed, and I knew he had never said some of those things, but I did not want to speak up. I had no idea things would go the way they did—-and so fast!

I was busy that day, when I heard that a trial had been called very quickly and Pilate had been bullied into having Jesus crucified. I had never been impressed with Pilate. He had no internal value system and could be pushed around so easily. I was really upset, but by the time I learned about it, it was too late to do anything. My sons came to me, quite agitated, saying that Jesus was dead, and we had to do something, right away! I calmed them down by agreeing that I would go to Pilate, because we knew each other professionally. I would ask if we could observe the Jewish rite of burial prior to the Sabbath. We could use our private family tomb on a temporary basis.

So I went to Pilate. I didn't tell him he was wrong in what he had done, or that I knew Jesus had never been a threat to Rome. There was no reason to take that risk at that point. I simply explained our Jewish customs and asked for custody of his body. Then I contacted Nicodemus, whom I knew was at least sympathetic to what Jesus was doing. He brought some burial spices, and we temporarily wrapped the body in a shroud and put it safely in the tomb.

I wish I could have done more. I probably should have, but I just didn't expect things to turn out the way they did.

—The story of Joseph of Arimathea is in Matthew 27:47–61 and Luke 25:50–60.

40. What Are We Doing Here?

When your father was a career military man in the Roman army, it is almost an automatic thing that you would follow him in your own career. That was the only life I had ever known, and it did have its benefits. How many people in my day have had the opportunity to live in seven different countries?

I was born a Roman citizen and have been a Roman soldier for thirty-five years. My wife is also a Roman citizen, born and raised in Greece. We met when I was stationed there. But neither of us has ever been to Rome, and I doubt we will ever get there.

I have been stationed in and around Palestine for the past twenty years. I have never risen in the ranks above being a regular soldier, and have seen more than my share of battlefield duty. I consider myself fortunate to be alive and have a wife and three children. My years in the service allow me some options in where I serve, and we plan to stay in Palestine.

Three years ago, I was assured permanent status as one of the temple guards in Jerusalem. It is a quiet, simple responsibility. My wife and I are not religious people. There are lots of gods in the Roman religious system, but we have never needed them, so we don't pay any attention to them.

That is why my assignment as an official guard at the Jewish temple is so interesting. I can stand off to the side and watch other people practice their religious beliefs. I don't understand Judaism. It has something to do with sacrificing animals and paying close attention to the blood. I just don't see how that is a religious thing. But on the other hand, I also see how much money goes through the temple, and some of it is used to feed the hungry and help the poor. These people do that because they believe their God wants them to do it. I guess that is OK, there are a lot of poor people here in Jerusalem.

Their religious faith has quite an impact on their lives, but I wish they would not be so angry with us. We are here to protect them. We keep the country stable so they can worship and live the way they want to live. We have a set policy. We do not interfere in the religious life of a nation as long as their religious practices do not challenge the authority of Rome.

After three years of daily duty at the temple, I have come to know some of the priests, and I recognize people who come regularly for worship. Their religious leaders do not want us to have any interaction with worshipers, so I stay in the background.

What do I do as a guard at the temple? I keep order. There are usually crowds here, and where you have a crowd, you have the inevitable thieves and other petty criminals. I have learned to spot troublemakers, and am pleased to report that in the last three years, we have had no "incidents" that required direct action. When I see something that looks even slightly suspicious, I simply go to that spot, and as my presence becomes known, I see some people leaving rather quickly. That is a good thing.

What other people forget or don't know is that the temple is more than just a place of worship. A lot of money changes hands here every day. There is quite a large bank inside the temple (with much more money in it than most people are aware of). There are several official money changers there who work with considerable amounts of money each day. It is good to have several Roman guards around to ensure their safety. I know that most of the people do not like my presence here, but the head priests, the bank officials and the money changers are awfully glad that we are here.

We did have some excitement here two days ago. A radical Jewish prophet figure came into the temple and created a minor riot that made a mess of the place. I immediately started toward the man who was causing the commotion and was ready to take action when the priest in charge that day stopped me, saying it was a temple matter that they would take care of. My standing orders were not to interfere in local matters, so I withdrew. It only lasted five or six minutes and it was over. I never really understood what the issue was, but within thirty minutes, everything was pretty well back to normal again.

This morning, a couple of my military colleagues casually reported that there were three crucifixions scheduled for this afternoon. That was not particularly unusual. It is a terrible shame that some people just don't know how to conduct themselves without getting into trouble. I learned that two of the prisoners are serious criminals while the third is some religious figure. I thought that was a bit unusual; Rome usually does not take such drastic measures with religious figures. We aren't into religious issues. But that's not my responsibility, so I paid no attention. There are a lot of crucifixions these days. This is a dangerous time.

My tour of duty at the temple ended at three in the afternoon, and I was glad to go back to camp. This would give me a long evening with my children.

But just after six, my commanding officer notified me that several of us from the temple duty team have been ordered to stand guard duty at some tomb. That was strange. Our orders were pretty vague: stand guard and make sure nothing happens at the tomb for three days. What did they think was going to happen? Other than the very rare grave robbers (who stole and then sold dead bodies), tombs are pretty dead places. (Sorry for the pun!)

But Octavian and I were assigned to move from temple duty to tomb duty for three days as part of a rotating assignment. We drew the Saturday evening to Sunday morning shift.

We arrived at the tomb about fifteen minutes early and were briefed by the two guards who were just completing their assignment. They told us what they knew about the situation. This was the religious figure who had been crucified on Friday. The chief priests did not want anything to go amiss. We joked about how boring this was going to be, and whether we had any games to play or stories to tell. The tomb was inside a garden wall that had a door at the entry. There was no way anyone would get in to this tomb. I thought temple duty was mundane; this seemed downright stupid to me.

On guard duty, you don't sit there staring at whatever it is you are guarding. That is not where any problems will come from. We first set up the perimeter of the garden, checked all the walls, gates, and other possible entry or exit routes. We built a fire, and started systematic, timed walks around the perimeter of garden. That was our ritual throughout the night.

It was very early in the morning, when suddenly the brightest light I had ever seen suddenly appeared over the tomb. It was very strange. The light was too bright to look at, but it did not cast any shadows or light up the garden. I looked at Octavian, but before I could speak, I felt all the strength draining from my body. Octavian was already in a pile on the ground, and I felt myself collapsing right beside him. I tried valiantly to get up, after all, I am a Roman soldier, but I could not move.

Then a second light came out of the tomb. It seemed to have a human shape, but it was too vague for me to be sure. How did that light get out of the tomb? I know that stone was sealed. I again tried to reach for my sword, but my arms wouldn't move. I tried to get up, but nothing in my body responded. All I could do was watch as the two brilliant lights went past us and out of the garden. They weren't walking; they were more like gliding along.

But my main concern was my own body. What had happened to me? Was I going to be paralyzed for life? It was maybe twenty or thirty minutes later that I started to feel a tingling in my arms and legs and I found I could move a bit. I also saw Octavian starting to get up. We finally got to our feet and took some wobbly steps toward the tomb. The stone was moved. I have no idea how that happened. The tomb was empty. What were those lights? What did they do? Where did the body go? I know that those strange, powerful lights were not carrying anything.

Octavian and I immediately went into soldier mode. We made a very quick check of the gates, the wall and the full perimeter. Nothing had been touched. We did a thorough inspection of the stone and the empty tomb. There was nothing there to indicate that anything had happened, except the body was gone and some rags were lying there. I assumed they had been wrapped around the body.

We had a big problem. We had been assigned to keep anything from happening at this tomb, and something drastic had happened. That is a serious matter for Roman soldiers on guard duty. We knew we had to report it, and I knew what the possible consequences might be for Octavian and myself. But we were required to report, so we went to our centurion and informed him of what had happened. He immediately sent a messenger to the high priests, demanding that they come to our headquarters. We gave the same report to them.

They were furious, and I don't blame them. We had an assignment and we had failed. They went off by themselves, talked privately, and then came back with a solution. We should say that we fell asleep, and while we were sleeping, some friends of this man came and stole the body.

I reacted immediately for two reasons. Falling asleep while on guard duty was one of the most serious crimes a soldier could commit. It carried the potential for the death penalty. I had not fallen asleep, and I was not about to die for something I did not do. And if we had fallen asleep, how would we have known who it was that stole the body? Their solution did not make sense, and I was not about to risk my life for these men whose religious beliefs meant nothing to me.

They met again, then came back and talked to my Centurion. They had a new offer. They would pay us a substantial amount of money if we would stick to their story. They agreed with our Centurion that no punishment would be meted out to us even if Pilate himself found out about it.

Our centurion pulled us aside and insisted we take the money and stick with the story. He promised to file a confidential report that would give our account. Our names would never be disclosed as being the guards on duty. That would protect us from any Roman judgment.

Octavian and I looked at each other. We just shrugged, took the money and went home. But I was very nervous for the next several weeks. I knew what had happened, and I still am not religious, but something far beyond my own understanding happened out there that night. I would love to know what it was, but I will not risk my future by asking questions. Only my wife knows my story, and we have told no one else. Not one single person.

—The story of the soldiers is in Matthew 27:62–66, 28:1–15.

41. Prove It!

Being the younger twin means you have to adjust in many ways. My twin sister Lydia was absolutely brilliant. She understood everything and trusted everyone. As a result, everyone loved her. Me? Well, I soon discovered I could not match her when it came to studying, so I decided to express myself in a different way. She believed everything, while I asked questions. She trusted people, while I told them they had to prove it to me. She instantly liked everyone she met, but when I met someone, I would wait to see what he or she was like before deciding whether or not we would be friends.

When I first met Jesus, I played my usual role. I listened, then went home to think about what he had said. I thought it was okay. Lydia was instantly enthralled. By the third time I heard Jesus, I was ready to accept what he was saying. I was surprised a few weeks later when Jesus invited me to join the group of disciples he was forming. It was like a tutor-student relationship. I told him I was not the smartest student in my class, but he said that didn't matter. If I wanted to be part of something bigger than myself, I should join the group. So I did. It wasn't a full-time thing. We would travel with Jesus, listen to him teach, then he would spend time with us explaining what it all meant.

It was certainly interesting, but I was always on the edge of the group. Leadership was not my style. I think I raised too many questions for the other disciples. Usually, after that happened, one of the disciples would quietly thank me for asking because he did not understand it either. I often felt like saying, "If you didn't understand, why didn't you ask? Why make me do it all the time?"

For example, one day, Jesus was talking about the future, and how he was going to prepare a place for us, and how we all knew how to get there. It sounded like a riddle to me, so I asked, "How can we know the way when we don't even know where you are going?" I think Lydia would have known exactly what Jesus meant, but I sure didn't. I smiled to myself when Philip asked a follow-up question, wanting Jesus to simplify what he meant so we could understand it. It was often that way. If I asked the first question, the others would ask their own questions, and we would then understand what Jesus was talking about.

There was another day when I spoke up. We had just received word that Lazarus was sick. We had a couple of days already planned, so Jesus said we would stay where we were and then visit Lazarus in a few days. In typical fashion, the other disciples weren't very eager about going. They reminded Jesus about the last time they had been in Bethany. Some of the Jews wanted to stone him, so why go back now? Jesus gave us a short lecture about loyalty, trust, and death. It was clear he was going regardless of what we thought, so I just blurted out, "If that is what you are going to do, we might as well go with you. Maybe they will stone us too. At least we can all die together." (None of the disciples thought my attempt at humor was very funny. They were an awfully serious bunch at times.)

We stayed with Jesus right up until the end. The last couple of days were unbelievably horrible. It was awful seeing what the Romans did to him. What was even worse, there was nothing we could do to stop it. Jesus would not let us defend him. Peter tried, and Jesus gave him a tongue-lashing for attacking that slave in Gethsemane.

At the cross, we stayed pretty much in the background. Rome often watched to see who came to crucifixions because that told them who else was a member of this criminal's gang. Thinking back, I am embarrassed that we left the women to stay right up there alone with Jesus until he was dead. We were so discouraged and frightened; we just wanted to get out of there alive.

A couple of days later, I was out on an errand. When I came back, the disciples had this absolutely preposterous story about how Jesus had come into the room with them. I right away wanted to know what was going on, because I knew I had locked the door when I left. They told me he had just appeared in the room.

"Yeah, sure, right through a locked door. You guys are living in a fantasy world." They insisted they had seen him, and they even described his bloody hands. That was more than I could accept, and my skeptical side kicked in. "Unless I see them for myself, and until I put my finger in the hole that sword made in his side, I'm not going to believe what you are saying. It makes no sense."

It turns out, they were right (at least this time). A week later, we were all together when Jesus appeared again. He looked at me and said, "Okay, Thomas, here I am. You want to touch the evidence? Go ahead." And with that he stuck out his hand. That did it. I didn't need any more proof. I was convinced. Jesus had one more thing to say.

"You believed because you saw the evidence. Can you imagine what it will be like for people to believe who don't have the privilege of seeing the evidence?"

I saw Jesus only one more time after that. We were in Galilee at a place where Jesus said he would meet us. It was an interesting experience because even there, some people had difficulty accepting that it really was Jesus. He gave us some final instructions, promised to always be with us, and he was gone.

Not long after that, we disciples were talking about what we were going to do next. I said I wanted to go east, back to the Jewish community living in Baghdad. I had relatives there. So that is what I did.

I wrote my own recollections of the life of Jesus. It really was a gospel of Jesus, but everybody called it the gospel of Thomas, so I let it stand at that. The message was there even if the title wasn't quite right.

—This Thomas story is in John 20:19–29

42. The Long Walk Home---Into Our Future

My wife and I were a devout Jewish couple who were faithful in our support of the local synagogue. When we got married, we immediately felt we wanted to do more than passively participate in religious life. We lived just outside Jerusalem, where I was a teacher in a Roman school, and my wife, Sharon, worked in the mission ministries of our synagogue. It was unusual to have a woman giving leadership to the relief ministry of the Synagogue. That had always been a man's position. In all honesty, it still was. That is, a man held the title of director, but everyone knew Sharon was the living inspiration that made the program a success.

She developed a program that provided clothing for the poor. She had contacts with more-prosperous Jewish families and even some Roman women. She persuaded them to donate their slightly worn clothing to the synagogue, where they employed widowed women as seamstresses to repair the robes and tunics before giving them to the poor. That led to a synagogue program of training women in sewing and cleaning so they could survive the tragedy of being widowed. There seemed to be a lot of Jewish widows in Jerusalem these days.

When I was not teaching, I was an avid student of our religious history and scriptures. I had thought about being a rabbi, but it never felt like the right time. By working as a teacher in a Jewish-Roman school, I had a better-than-average income, and I was able to influence a better understanding between Jewish and Roman young people. I did not like the Roman military, but there were many other Roman families who served in support roles without actually being part of the military. Some of them were our neighbors, so we were friends. But we quietly never lost the hope that someday our country would be free from occupation troops and we would be our own nation.

I loved our local synagogue. Even though Sharon and I went to the temple several times a year for the festivals, I never had the same experience there as I did in the smaller synagogue setting. There was too much ritual and too much money involved in temple worship. But that was where we first met a young prophet/teacher named John. We had known his parents, Zechariah and Elizabeth, but we had lost contact with their son, John, until he began a pretty radical preaching and teaching ministry. As an adult student of faith, I was able to listen to John with some theological understanding. He was clearly different. He reminded me of Isaiah, Amos, and Micah all rolled into one.

It was my wife who first got me involved with John. In her work with the poor, she heard a distinct tone in John's preaching that resonated with what she was doing. I really liked his vision for the future and his call to a faith that made a difference. Sharon and I found our own faith being challenged and strengthened and we soon were involved with a group of people who were active followers of this John the Baptist.

But then another voice began to be heard across the countryside. John's cousin Jesus was also starting to preach and teach. We were there one day at the Jordan River, where John was teaching, when Jesus came and asked to be baptized. It was an interesting exchange. John wasn't sure he should do it, but Jesus insisted. It had a certain kind of drama and excitement to it. John had baptized lots of people, but this was different. John told the small crowd, "This is the one whom God is going to use. This is the man whom I also want to follow. Listen to him. He is the voice of God for our day."

That was quite an introduction, but Sharon and I stayed with John. We were not critical of Jesus; we just stayed with John. But then tragedy struck. John was arrested and put in jail. With my Roman connections at the school, I was allowed a rare visit. John asked me to make contact with Jesus to be sure Jesus was really the one we were expecting to bring new life to Israel.

So I contacted Jesus, asked my question, and got a strange answer. Jesus told me to tell John what he was doing, and he provided a whole list of things that impacted the poor, the sick, and the oppressed. He told me to urge John to adjust his vision of what he was expecting from the Messiah.

I was impressed. When I reported to John, John agreed. He urged me that if anything happened to him to give my support to Jesus. Well, John was murdered by Herod not long after that, so Sharon and I switched our loyalties to Jesus. The more I heard, the more I was convinced by what Jesus was doing. We and some of our friends became very active in supporting Jesus. It was a natural for Sharon because her work at the synagogue fit so neatly into what Jesus was teaching.

That lasted nearly three years. And they were wonderful, exciting years. By then, we were very familiar with the themes Jesus was preaching. We traveled with him once in a while, meeting with other groups as they learned about Jesus. We were sure that in Jesus, a new day was coming for us and for

Israel. The crowds were getting bigger, and the excitement was getting more intense. Sharon saw a definite increase in interest at the synagogue mission. More people were bringing in clothes; and more people wanted to help in whatever way they could. This new day Jesus was talking about was being experienced all around us. We had dreams about how all this would change our lives forever. I knew the Old Testament prophets. I could see, this was the new day they said would come with the promised Messiah, and we were part of it. It was wonderful!

And then our dreams were shattered in the space of three days. A lifetime of building and working for the future, and in three days it was absolutely gone. Like John before him, Jesus was arrested, and before we had any chance to come to his aid, Rome had executed him without even making it clear what he had done.

We were staying with friends in Jerusalem because it was Passover, but how do you celebrate when all hope has been taken from your life? We stayed through the Sabbath, then on the first day of the week, Sharon and I said our good-byes and headed for our home in Emmaus. This time, we walked by ourselves because we simply had no energy to walk with anyone else. As we walked, we reminisced about the way it felt when Jesus was preaching. We remembered that time when he fed the five thousand. How could that have been seen as a threat to anybody? We tried to make sense of it all, but it just didn't come. There was nothing right about what had just happened. We tried to think about what we would do now, but we did not have the energy to even think about the future.

We heard footsteps coming up behind us, and Sharon slid closer to me. There were only the two of us, and who knew who this person was or what he might want? But he fell in step with us, and we walked quietly for a few minutes before he asked what was wrong. He said we seemed sad, and it was Passover festival time. We made a couple of very general comments, and he seemed interested. So we told him about what had happened and how it just ripped the life right out of us.

Then he began to talk, and I remember thinking that he must be a rabbi, because he gave us a quick summary of Torah theology about how to understand the role of the Messiah and how almost all the great prophet figures in Israel had been killed by the authorities. It was so exciting. I knew my Torah and I knew the prophets, and I began asking questions. He answered them quietly, calmly, and with true wisdom. It was a fantastic tutorial in prophetic promises. I could feel my heart beating faster and faster as we walked.

Before we knew it, we were home. We urged him to come in and stay with us because I had many more questions. He responded to us in such a warm, friendly spirit. It was as though we had known each other a long time.

Sharon set out some bread and wine on the table. I reached for the bread, expecting to offer a prayer and share it with our guest. But he already had the bread in his hands, and he began to pray; soft, simple words that expressed perfectly what we had felt on the road. I felt a rush come over me because I knew I had heard those words before. I opened my eyes and stared. Our guest broke off a piece of bread and handed it to me. And then I saw ... *It was him!* How could I not have realized that before? We had walked for several miles, but I had been so wrapped up in my own grief that I did not see who was walking with us.

He had the slightest smile on his face as if he was enjoying the moment of our surprise. When I blinked, he was gone. I looked at Sharon. She was staring wide eyed at the bread. "Did you see what I just saw?" I asked. She just nodded her head. What was there to say? I looked at her. "We have to tell the disciples." She was already on her feet heading for the door. We ran and walked and walked and ran all the way back to Jerusalem. "Tell me I'm not dreaming," Sharon said at one point when we paused to catch our breath. "Did you hear what he told us on the road?" I asked at another pause. And then we would run again.

Our world had not ended. Our dreams had been given new life. Tomorrow will be another day, and then there will be another one and another one after that. Our life is not tied to something that was done to Jesus. Our hope is in what Jesus was doing.

We will go back to remember the events of that Passover weekend, but we will keep moving forward, for that is where Jesus is to be found in our lives.

Our story has not ended. It is just beginning.

—The story of Cleopas and his wife is in Luke 24:13–35.

43. Mark—A Man on the Edge

It feels like I have known Jesus all my life. I was born and raised in Jerusalem, and my parents were involved in many of the things that happened during his ministry.

I did not meet him until he became more widely known as a teacher and rabbi. My mother knew his family, and as a devout Jewish woman, she was intrigued by his handling of scripture, his friendliness with people, and his quiet confidence.

But I am getting ahead of myself. My father died when I was a young boy, so I grew up learning how to be responsible around the house and to help with the family fishing business. The loss of my father was a significant blow but not a catastrophe; we knew it was coming for the last year of his life. Thus, my mother was quite prepared to take over the family business. We were fortunate to have my cousin Barnabas living close to us, and he provided supervision and counsel to keep everything going smoothly.

We had several boats, which meant a sizeable crew. They were very loyal to my mother, and she paid them well, so that part of our lives was secure. That meant that we were able to keep a house that was larger than most. My mother had a young girl, Rhoda, to assist with that part of our lives so Mother could spend more time with the family business.

Certainly we missed my father. But with just a bit of reorganization, we once again were running a successful fishing business that provided very well for us. It was inevitable that I would go to synagogue school, and also be trained in fishing, reading, and religion.

I was a teenager when I met Jesus. It was strange how that happened. When you are in the fishing business, people know each other, and we generally got along quite well. On one occasion, Peter wanted to have dinner for a group of fishing friends to hear a new rabbi who was creating quite a stir. His home was not big enough for the twenty friends he wanted to include, so he asked if our house would be available to host the dinner. We had done things like this before, so of course Mother said yes. I was glad she did because this gave me the chance to sit along the wall and listen to the conversation between Jesus, Peter, and his personal group of friends.

Jesus was truly exciting. The way he read and talked about the Torah was so stimulating. He even answered the questions I was having in synagogue school about God and what God's vision was for our people. Though I was young, I wanted to hear more even though the rabbis at my synagogue school downplayed this rabbi's approach to the Law.

Over the next two years, our house became an informal gathering place for a growing group of people who were supporting this young rabbi Jesus. I was never really part of the official group, but they would let me sit around the edges and listen to their conversation. I learned all I could and followed closely what Jesus said, where he went, and what the common reactions were.

I sensed there was some tension between Jesus and the traditional religious leaders in Jerusalem. My teachers at the synagogue were not all of one mind. Some felt Jesus was too radical and would cause trouble. Others were more positive about him, and some of them even came to our house at times to join the Jesus conversations.

It was no surprise to me when Mother started planning to have the Passover meal for Jesus and his disciples. We had done this twice before. It was not a simple task, because while the men ate upstairs, the women and children enjoyed a good meal in our family kitchen and dining area. I learned about this when mother sent me to get water from the well. One of the disciples met me on the road and asked about using our second-story room for Passover. I knew Mother had talked about it, so I told him we were getting everything ready.

When everyone came, they went upstairs, and I was permitted to go with them to act as host. I got to hear the conversation. It seems there was a bit of tension in the room after the meal. One man who had been sitting next to Jesus got up and left in a hurry. I did not understand what was going on, but it wasn't my place to worry about that.

But I did hear one of them say they were going to Gethsemane after the meal. That was not far from our house, so after the cleaning up was finished, I went to Gethsemane just to be part of the group. I will never forget what happened there. I have never been as terrified as I was that night. Not much was going on. In fact, most of the disciples were sleeping half the time as they waited for Jesus to come back from his private time of prayer.

That was when I heard the crowd coming. I stepped back into the bushes, hiding so I could watch without being seen. A group was being led by the man who had left the dinner so quickly. I counted three Roman soldiers and about twelve to fifteen Jewish men. There was something wrong. Several of the men had swords. That told me they probably were zealots.

Then I saw Jesus coming back. He gathered the disciples, and they started down the path toward the crowd. Somehow, a fight broke out. I could not see who started it, but I saw Peter take a wild swing with a sword. Why he had that sword I do not know. Roman law did not allow Jewish people to carry swords. I had never seen any of the disciples with a sword. There was a shrill scream, and everything got really quiet. I heard people running away, but Jesus was bent over, paying attention to the man who was lying on the ground. The next thing I saw was the soldiers grab Jesus and half-drag him down the path.

When I gasped in surprise, one of the soldiers heard me and started toward me. I took off running, but he caught me by the sleeve. He wanted to know who I was and what I was doing out there. I have never been so scared. I wriggled out of my robe and ran for home as fast as I could. I was glad it was dark, because I didn't have anything on!

I woke up late the next morning and found my mother crying. She told me that Jesus had been arrested last night, the Sanhedrin had met, and Pilate had sentenced Jesus to death. She knew that Jesus' mother was staying with Barnabas, so she was going there to find out what was going on. She gave me strict orders not to leave the house. What was happening was not something I needed to see.

So I missed the crucifixion of Jesus. Mother didn't talk about it when she got home. She was literally shaking and could hardly talk. She said it had been the most gruesome, sickening thing she had ever seen. She and several others became physically sick when they saw what those soldiers did to Jesus. How can human beings be so cruel to another human being?

Later that day, one of the disciples—I think it was Andrew—stopped at the house and told us that Jesus was dead. He also told us that a wealthy Jewish man had taken the body off the cross so that it could be buried before the Sabbath started. Mother asked where this man lived, and when Andrew told her, I recognized the address. We regularly delivered fish to that family. He was a good man, a well-respected Jewish leader.

With that, the pall of death settled over our family. There is a kind of silence about death that is different from just having an absence of noise or conversation. Very little was said, and what was said was in whispered tones. We observed the rituals of Passover, but it was different. A tragedy had struck our lives and it penetrated the heart of our souls. It was more than the loss of a friend, as bad as that was. This was the loss of our future, our vision, our hope that had been building for three years. In less than one day, it was gone. Would life ever be the same again for us?

The next morning, two women came to the house and talked with mother. I heard them say something about how they should help Mary clean up the body and arrange for proper burial. They did not want to leave that to Jesus' mother. That would be such an awful thing to have to do after seeing him die like he did.

The Mark story is in the gospel of Mark 14 – 15.

44. Mark Moves to the Middle

That Sabbath was one of the longest days of my life. Normally, Sabbath was a time for reflection, study of the Torah, and relaxation. But when you are in a home that has been devastated by events that have wiped out years of hoping and dreaming, you don't do much except sit around and think about how you had expected it to be so different. You end up hoping you could just back up a day and discover that yesterday had never happened.

I woke up very early the next morning. It was Sunday, the start of our work week. I decided to visit the tomb where they had taken Jesus' body. In my short years of knowing him, I had discovered that being near him gave me a sense of confidence and hope. I know it doesn't make logical sense, but I felt I might get some comfort just by being close to him again even if it was only his dead body. The sun was not up yet, and it was quite dark, but I knew my way around this part of Jerusalem. It took only ten minutes to get to the Arimathea property.

The area around the private tomb was an open space, and right away, I noticed something was wrong. The stone was not covering the entrance to the tomb. Tombs had to be secure for protection of the body. I went closer to get a good look. I could see no sign of tampering. It was just open as if it had never been closed. I looked around, saw nobody, so I went into the tomb. I had no idea what I was expecting to find except the dead body of Jesus, but it wasn't there. That didn't make sense. There was a bench on the side that had a blanket or robe lying on it but nothing more. No body. Nothing! I sat down on the bench and tried to figure out what was going on.

That was when I saw them coming. Mary Magdalene, whom I barely knew, Salome, whom I knew only by name, and Mary, the mother of James, were coming into the garden. I expected my mother to be with them, but she wasn't. It was still dark inside the tomb, so they didn't recognize me. I pointed to the empty bench and said, "Look. The body is gone. That's where they laid him. I don't know any more than that." They took one long look, put down the things they were carrying, and left in a hurry.

The sun was starting to come up, so I went home too. It was not until later in the day, when a few people came to our house to tell my mother Jesus was not in the tomb that I told her where I had been, and what I had seen. The tomb was empty, but I hadn't seen anything else.

Then things got hectic. Cleopas and his wife came to our house, saying they were on their way home to Emmaus when Jesus had come up behind them and had walked with them for about three miles. Then Peter burst in through the door saying he had seen Jesus. What more was going to happen?

By now most of the disciples were upstairs, and together, we tried to make sense of it all when we got the absolute shock of our lives. Jesus appeared out of nowhere and was standing at the door. He wondered why we were all so surprised. He talked for just a few minutes. Then he was gone again!

For the next ten to fifteen years, the whole group took a lot of energy from those few minutes. People who had heard Jesus became followers, and we met regularly for worship. We shared stories about how we remembered what Jesus had said or done. We tried to keep alive the things that Jesus had taught us about what God wanted. For me, life returned to normal because I had work to do, but I never forgot what happened that day at our house.

It was fifteen or sixteen years after that day that my cousin Barnabas came asking to talk with me and my mother. He and his good friend Paul had felt strongly that they should go over into Cyprus and other regions with the story of Jesus and what had happened. They knew a few people on Cyprus who were followers of Jesus, and they wanted to do the kind of thing Jesus had done so often, just go and engage people in conversation about faith and how we should live. They would tell the stories of Jesus and encourage people to join with us in being followers of Jesus.

I had never married—no great reason, just never did—so I was more free to do things like that. I immediately said I would go, and a week later, Barnabas, Paul, and I left for Cyprus. Cyprus was a big island about sixty miles out in the Mediterranean Sea. It was about 30 to 40 percent Jewish, the rest Gentile. Because he was widely known as a rabbi, Paul was invited to speak in the synagogues. He told people about what Jesus had taught and what had happened. Quite a few people liked what Paul said, and they began meeting to talk about following Jesus.

After about two weeks on Cyprus, I thought we would probably head back to Jerusalem. But Paul and Barnabas began talking about going up into Asia and some of the places where Paul had lived as a young man. That was a new idea for me. I knew Jesus had spoken about the renewal of our Jewish faith. Now Paul and my cousin Barnabas were going to go into solidly Gentile territory. They had not talked about doing that when we first started out. Jesus was Jewish, our common faith was Jewish, and I felt we should keep it that way. It was quite all right to talk with Gentile people who came to our synagogues, but it was something quite different to go into a Gentile nation and take the initiative in talking with Gentiles.

I told Paul and Barnabas how I felt, and we had a long argument about it. I knew what the Law said about interacting with Gentiles, but Paul and Barnabas said we are living in a new day. They were committed to going to Asia, so I told them, "Fine, but you can go by yourselves. I am not going with you. I do not believe Jesus would approve of this."

So I went back to Jerusalem. When the group leaders asked me why I had come home without Paul and Barnabas, I told them exactly how I felt about what Barnabas and Paul were doing.

It was six or eight months later when Paul and Barnabas came home. They had lots of stories to tell about how Gentiles were accepting the ideas that Jesus had about God's new way of living. People were leaving their Greek gods and were serious about Jesus and his message. They were quite excited about the success they had had.

Several times over the next months, Barnabas talked with me about why I had left them in Cyprus, and I began to realize how he felt and even began to see the need to reach out to Gentiles with the Jesus story. It took a while, but gradually I changed as I thought about how the message of Jesus applied to others as well. But Paul and I never got things worked out. We talked a couple of times, but I don't think Paul liked me very much.

Two years later, Barnabas stopped by the house and asked if I would consider going with Paul and him on another mission trip. They wanted to visit all the places they had been before and just talk with these new followers of Jesus. By now, I was solidly with Barnabas on the Gentile thing, and I instantly said I would be glad to go. But the next day, Barnabas came back with bad news. He and Paul had a really big fight over me. Paul was very clear. I was not going to be included on this trip.

Barnabas said he tried to explain that I had changed, but Paul would not listen. It got so bad that Paul even refused to take Barnabas with him. He told Barnabas to stay home, that he would take Silas instead. I knew that Barnabas felt really bad about the whole thing because he did want to go on another trip, so I suggested that we go together. We could go back to Cyprus. Let Paul and Silas go to Greece if they wanted to. So that is what we did, but both of us felt kind of bad about parting company with Paul on not very good terms.

Barnabas and I had a good trip. We made a good team. I had been around Jesus for much of his ministry, and I knew a lot of the details about what had happened. People were glad to see us, and it was an exciting adventure. After a week on Cyprus, I could tell Barnabas wanted to keep going, so I even suggested, "Let's go to Greece. I think I'm ready." Barnabas was very pleased. He told me about a man he wanted me to meet at Colosse, a man named Philemon.

Going into Asia Minor was good for me. We had opportunities to talk with Gentiles who were already members of the Jewish faith and had heard just a bit about what Jesus had taught. We could fill them in on a lot more things, and they found that exciting. We kept moving and got to Colosse. Imagine our surprise when we went to the house of Philemon and found Paul staying there for a few days. It was kind of tense at first, but Paul and I had a couple of long talks. I apologized to Paul for leaving them in Cyprus. I explained how Barnabas had helped me think in some new ways. I told him of the excitement I felt when Gentiles actually wanted to know about Jesus. Paul finally accepted Barnabas's good word on my behalf, and we became friends again. I was glad for that, because I felt really badly about how I had left them three years ago on Cyprus.

Barnabas and I left Colosse and headed for Jerusalem, where I began traveling with Peter as a storyteller to confirm details about the life of Jesus. I had lived through most of these events, so I knew them well. For three or four years, Peter and I were the "storytellers of the faith." I would tell about something that had happened, then Peter would explain what it meant and how people should respond. Together, the two of us covered most of the public life of Jesus several times over.

But sadly, in the meantime, things had not gone so well with Paul. He had come back to Jerusalem, where he was arrested on some mistaken charges brought by a few radical, conservative Jews. We tried to keep in touch, but he dropped out of sight for over two years. I knew he had gone back toward Greece and was hoping to get to Rome, but then, we heard he was in prison for nearly two years in Asia before being transferred to Rome. We were friends, at least sort of, but I certainly was not expecting to get word from Paul asking if I would join him in Rome. He said he needed me to help tell the stories of Jesus. He reminded me that during the life and ministry of Jesus, he and Jesus were not on the same side! Most people never got to see Paul's subtle sense of humor, but he had one!

So I was in Rome with Paul for about a year before returning to Jerusalem. In a way, I was fortunate to have left Rome when I did. Not long after I left the city, Nero threw all the Christians he could find in jail and had most of them killed. We were not surprised to learn that Paul had been among them. Paul never was one to stay in the shadows to protect himself. But the really tragic thing was that Peter had gone to Rome to visit Paul, and he got caught in that same Nero purge. He was simply in the wrong place at the wrong time, and it cost him his life. That hit me hard, because Peter was the closest friend I had ever had.

Now he was gone. Peter had been closer to Jesus than any of the other disciples. People had trusted what Peter had said, and now he was dead. Who was going to pick up the task of telling the stories of Jesus?

It was after one of our followers-of-Jesus worship meetings that three of the group leaders stopped me on the way out. "Mark," they said, "you were around as a boy for most of what happened to Jesus in Jerusalem. You saw it. You were a close friend of Peter for years, and you know the stories he told and how he explained what it all meant. You have to write these things down before they get lost. Already, people are telling stories that we know are not true. You must help us put together a record of the things Jesus did. You know more than any of us about what happened. You have got to do it."

So I spent three years putting stories together, trying to organize what I remembered, and what I could recall Peter saying. I tried to be careful about what I wrote. I gave it to the followers-of-Jesus group at Antioch. I do not know what happened to it after that. I hope people actually did read it. I also hope that it was helpful for some people. I never found out.

Author's note:

This is Mark's story. We do not know what happened to Mark. There is no record of where he lived or when he died. Some scholars believe he stayed in Jerusalem, which was his childhood home, and died in the Jewish revolt of CE 70, when Rome destroyed the temple and caused massive destruction to the city.

It is doubtful that Mark ever knew that both Matthew and Luke (whom he may have known only slightly) relied heavily on his writing when they wrote their own accounts of the life and teachings of Jesus. We owe Mark a lot of credit for many of the things we know about Jesus.

This Mark story is found in Mark 16, and in the Acts of the Apostles

45. Even Death Has Power

Have you ever tried to live in two cultures? It has its advantages, but it also makes it difficult to know exactly where you belong. I was born into a well-educated Greek family that saw the cultural advantages of the Greek world. But my parents had seen the advantages of the Jewish faith with its high moral and ethical values, its emphasis upon monotheism, and its strong religious history. They had become God fearers, meaning that we lived and worshipped within Jewish customs, but we had retained our Greek heritage. Thus, we straddled the two cultures, trying to draw from the best of each.

As regular participants in the synagogue, my parents saw the Torah as a helpful guide for how they lived. It was no secret that they had more progressive ideas about relating to other cultures and applying the Law in more creative ways. They were also active in ministry to the poor. We identified ourselves as Hellenists, Greek people who had accepted Jewish religious principles while retaining the Greek culture.

We were just becoming familiar with the Jesus message when he was crucified. That was a major shock for my parents; they had been hoping that what Jesus was saying would become the guiding principles of Jewish faith. They had a hard time believing that Jewish people could be so upset with Jesus that they would want to silence the voice of renewal and vitality in our faith.

After the crucifixion, our family stopped going to synagogue and began meeting with a small group of Jewish people who had been active with Jesus during his brief ministry. In my own education, I had gone through some extensive studies in Jewish history. My parents believed that knowledge of Jewish history and faith would be much more helpful for me than to be thinking about all the Greek gods.

We were quickly accepted by this new religious community. We had no organization or structure; we just met to tell the stories of Jesus and to reflect on how these were the fulfillment of the prophecies from our history. But it was not long until problems arose. We had quite a few older people who had little or no income, making their lives quite difficult. It was made even worse because the traditional Jewish community had cut off all the people who were followers of Jesus from the welfare services they had been receiving.

Our new community was trying to establish a system of care that would provide for these people patterned after the Jewish system. With our rapidly increasing numbers, the system was not precise enough, and people were being missed in the weekly food distribution. That is not unusual in the formation of a new system, but we began to notice something very disturbing. The Jewish widows were being well cared for, but the Greek widows were frequently missed, and that caused them to have a difficult time. I put together some data on what was happening and took this information to the leaders, who were unaware of it. They saw the problem, called the group together, and we tried to determine what should be done.

Seven of us were given the responsibility of seeing that the food distribution was fair and that all the appropriate persons were treated fairly. I was selected as one of the seven, and the new system worked quite well. That put me in a position of leadership in the community, and I began to serve as a teacher and spokesperson for the larger group. My training in Jewish religious history and in Greek public speaking made that an easy task.

At times, it was my responsibility to speak for the group in conversations with people who objected to who we were and what we believed. I enjoyed those encounters, because I knew my history and I was thoroughly familiar with what Jesus had been teaching.

I had always assumed that religious people would be straightforward and honest in what they said. I knew we might disagree on what something meant, but I trusted we would represent fairly what another person had said. That is how the trouble started. Some Jewish people refused to accept any truth except their own. That meant they twisted what we were saying so they could attack it and then also attack me.

There was very little room to talk together. A group came to our house one day and simply took me by force to meet with the Jewish council. I had been given no warning, and suddenly, there I was before a very hostile Sanhedrin, having to answer for things I had not said, and even for things Jesus had not said.

The high priest asked me point blank, "Are these things true? Is this what you are saying?" That seemed like a fair question, so I asked if I might respond. When they said yes, I walked them through their own religious history. After all, that is what I had been trained in, and I knew it quite well.

I gave them an extended lecture on Jewish history, carefully selecting those experiences that documented what I wanted to say. I touched on all the important persons and events. I began with the patriarchs, told how God had led us out of Egypt, and gave a lot of attention to Moses and the Torah. I went through our history to demonstrate how God had often tried to help us do what was right and how we had seldom if ever gotten the message. I quoted the Torah and the prophets, trying as best I could to get them to see their own history and how wrong they were to have killed Jesus.

I knew they would not like that, but someone had to say it because it was the truth. But I was not expecting the fury they directed at me. I thought this was a serious, thinking body of educated men who should be able to listen and respond with questions or other challenges. I would have liked that. That was what I had been expecting.

But as they began shouting at me, I saw the strangest thing. It was as though I saw through a window into heaven and saw Jesus. I know it was just in my head, but I declare I heard him say, "Stephen, you did well. You got it right. I am very pleased with you."

I have never had an experience like that before. It was so powerful and so personal. I could not help myself. I yelled my response, "Thank you Lord, I see you, I believe!"

That was when I was suddenly grabbed by a couple of men who dragged me outside. The only thing I saw was a man standing off to the side who appeared to be very angry. He seemed to be urging them on, and that was when the first stone hit me.

Stephen did not know it then, but the man standing there was Saul. Many people believe this was the beginning of the turning point in his life. He heard Stephen's interpretation of Jewish history, and it made a profound impact upon him. His initial response was a series of violent attacks on the followers of Jesus where he tried to silence anyone who dared speak in favor of this new understanding of history before he also "met" Jesus.

It is truly sad that it took Stephen's death to start this process for Paul because Stephen and Paul would have made a powerful team. Both were well educated and very articulate. Both were truly spiritual, godly persons with strong faith. Both had a similar vision of a faith that went far beyond traditional Jewish faith to include all people. Perhaps the lesson for us is that even in death, our faith has power to challenge the lives of other people.

—The story of Stephen's death is in Acts 6 and 7.

46. Don't Ask Me to do That

The Torah was my favorite subject. It was fascinating. It held such positive hope for anyone who takes it seriously. I know some people see it as burdensome with all its details and seemingly endless instructions about small things. I see that as a sign of God's care about every detail of our lives.

Being a teacher in the Synagogue without being a rabbi might seem strange, but it was logical for me. Digging around in the old texts was exciting. Finding where specific ideas in the Torah first emerged, then seeing how ideas grew and changed over the years gave meaning to my work. I might sound like a conservative person, always digging in the past, wanting to be faithful to the ways we used to do things. But that was not me. As I studied the history of Torah observance and interpretation, I saw how changes led to improvements in how we worshiped God and lived our faith.

Rabbi Hillel had always been my hero. He taught me that being faithful to the Torah doesn't necessarily mean doing everything exactly the way we always did it. It was exciting to discover how a new understanding often recovered the original meaning of the Torah, while leading to more creative applications.

That is why Jesus was so appealing to me. When I first heard him, I went straight back to my little work space at Gamaliel's School of the Torah, and did some checking. His interpretation of some important portions of the Torah had the ring of truth. His call to love enemies as much as friends was solidly rooted in a detail from Leviticus that had either been lost or at least neglected. Over the years we had adapted that teaching to allow us to hate enemies. That is not what the Torah originally intended.

That initial discovery got me excited, so I began checking some other things. Jesus said he was not trying to destroy the Law, but to fulfill it. If that was true, then I should be able to find a precedent for what he was saying. To my delight, I found Jesus was right again and again, about swearing oaths, about retaliation, about adultery, about divorce, and a lot of other things. He was exactly right in what he was teaching. The Torah had gradually been bent and twisted ever so slightly. It only sounded like he was being critical of the

Torah. He actually was trying to recover God's original intentions when He gave it to Moses.

That did it for me. I became a committed follower of Jesus almost from the very beginning. His message was exciting and liberating, yet faithful to everything God had given us. I was pleased to be able to contribute to his ministry in a special way. People often had questions about specific things Jesus said. Usually these questions came because traditional Jewish leaders felt challenged by how Jesus read the scriptures. I could offer clarification of what Jesus was saying, showing how his interpretation was solidly grounded in what the Torah really taught.

This created huge problems with the temple priests and the Sanhedrin. They insisted on staying with their understandings, assuming that their reading was the original message. I don't like to argue, so I seldom got involved in face to face encounters, but I was able to clarify things for other followers of Jesus who simply wanted more information.

I am not certain, but I think that is why Saul targeted me on his list of the enemies of Judaism. I was a threat because I provided detailed evidence supporting what Jesus had been teaching. I was never a leader of the new faith community in any official way, but people did trust me. Peter or James often asked me to explain something to the group. So I can understand how Saul might have believed I was a leader.

I was shocked when several members of the group came to me saying I had to get out of Jerusalem right away. They told me Saul had presented my name to the Sanhedrin as a follower of Jesus who had to be stopped because I was destroying what Jewish faith had always believed. I knew that was not true, and since I was not a public speaker I never expected he would come after me. After all, my life was devoted to a faithful reading and application of the Torah. I challenged my friends at first, but they were very insistent, so the next day my wife and I left for Damascus. I had family there, and there was a good Torah library where I could continue my work.

Leaving your whole life behind, all your friends, and all the familiar things that make life comfortable and easy was hard to do. I like traditional patterns, and I don't take risks very quickly. But we settled down in Damascus and became part of the followers of Jesus group that met there regularly.

We felt safe from Saul. We had told only a few very close friends in our faith group where we were going. I had no public role in the followers of Jesus group in Damascus.

I awoke one night in a panic. I was having a dream, or a vision, I could not tell which, but it was very real. God was telling me that Saul was in Damascus, staying in a house owned by a man named Judas. This house was only a very short walk from where we were living. I knew about Judas. He was a dominant person, quite outspokenly critical of anyone who said anything positive about Jesus. In my vision, the Lord told me to go to that house and meet with Saul. That was when I sat straight up in bed--meet with Saul? Saul wanted to have me arrested, why would I walk right into his hands?

"Lord, I am willing to do anything you ask. You know that, but don't ask me to do this!" But the vision continued, telling me that Saul was God's chosen messenger, and I need you to meet him and help him. Go. Right now!

What would you do? I turned to my wife. She was awake, startled by my sitting up with such a violent reaction. She thought I should listen to the vision. It sounded authentic to her. I got up, dressed, and asked her to pray for me as I went. I told her, "You know where I am going. If I don't come back, get some friends and come find me."

I met Saul, introduced myself, and told him why I had come. He seemed genuinely relieved to meet me. I explained to Saul that I was going to pray for him and lay my hands on his head to symbolize the anointing of God's Holy Spirit. As I reached toward Saul I saw that my hands were shaking uncontrollably and I couldn't stop them. When I put them on Saul's head it helped me calm down, and I began to pray. Don't ask me what I prayed because I don't remember. But as I prayed a strange, powerful peace came over me and I could feel the tension draining from my body.

When I ended the prayer, Saul looked up at me and opened his eyes. He told me what had happened two days ago as he was coming to Damascus. He focused on the part where he saw Jesus and I believed him. Even Judas was affected by this. He got some food for us, and we talked for several hours. I told Saul had I had checked the things that Jesus had taught. We talked about what the Jesus message was all about, and what it would mean for Israel. Saul asked good questions. He pushed hard, but I could tell he was hearing me.

That night was different from any night I have ever had. It was an experience I won't ever forget. What I did was so unlike me, but it was the right thing to do. I have always been thankful that I did it.

Saul and I agreed that I would meet with the faith community in Damascus, explain what had happened, and introduce them to Saul. We agreed that I should do that without Saul being there, because we felt his presence would frighten them too badly. That meeting went well, and the group agreed to meet with Saul, although not everyone was comfortable with the decision.

The next day Saul went to the synagogue telling people that he had met Jesus, and that he now believed that Jesus really was the Christ. With his persuasive logic and public speaking ability, a lot of people believed him. It was truly amazing. What made me really feel good was that Saul took a lot of the things he and I had talked about that first night, put them in his own words and turned them into a very persuasive argument for Jesus.

Some of the Jews who were expecting Saul to arrest those of us who followed Jesus got very angry at Saul. They called him a traitor and rumors quickly circulating that a few of them would try to kill him. We secretly hustled Saul out of the city that night and told him to go back to Jerusalem. I gave him the name of Barnabas, and how to contact him. Two members of our own group decided to travel with him for his own safety.

I have thought about that night often. Why did God choose me of all people? This was so out of character for me. I would have been no match for Saul if he had wanted to argue or debate with me. I had no idea what I was getting into as I walked to that house that night. In a way I was terribly frightened, but I was not nervous. How can that be? What if I would have decided not to go? That was my first sense. God should ask somebody else who is better at these things!

I am glad I went. If God ever asks me to do something again I hope I will have the courage to say "Yes, Lord, Here I am".

The story of Ananias is in Acts 9:10-25.

47. I Forgot to Open the Gate

I guess I will always be known as a maid, but that is not how it was in Mary's household. We were a fishing family, and we did not have maids or other servants. Mary would not have accepted that designation for me. Let me tell you how I came to be a member of this family.

I was born to Enos and Sarah. They were good parents, and we had a good family. We were poor but not much poorer than anyone else in our town. My father was a fisherman who had a small boat with a crew of three. I was an only child who came along a little later in life. I knew I was loved as a child, and I was given every opportunity my parents could afford.

I was twelve years old when it happened. We don't know what caused it exactly, but a sudden storm came up on the Sea of Galilee and my father's boat was lost. All four men on board were lost. That happened more often than most people knew. The larger boats could handle these storms, and those boats usually fished close to each other, so there was always help available. But my father had a smaller boat, and he fished alone. We knew there was risk involved, but he had assured us he knew how to handle Galilean storms.

I remember that day so vividly. I asked my mother if Father was safe because the wind off the sea was so fierce and the storm clouds were especially dark and turbulent. Being a fishing family, we learned at a very young age how to read the storm clouds. Mother assured me that I should not worry, that Father was a very skilled fisherman. He would be home soon.

But he didn't come home. That evening, as Mother and I were becoming more concerned, Aaron, whose boat was always tethered right next to my father's, came telling us that my father's boat had not come in. He said there was real fear that Father had been lost in the storm. Several other boats were waiting for the winds to die down so they could search for Father's boat.

Mother and I could not sleep that night. The sun was just coming up when Aaron came again and told us they had found nothing. The boat must have broken up in the storm. They found a few pieces of wood, but that was all. Enos must have drowned in the storm, he said. He was very sorry.

We always knew that kind of news was possible. Fishing was a dangerous occupation, but you never think it would happen to you. We never recovered Father's body, so we buried a few things that belonged to him. That gave us a place to go when we wanted to remember him.

But now, Mother had to face the issue of what we were going to do. A mother and daughter without a husband or father face a very bleak future. I remember the despair in my mother's face and the obvious pain she felt as she moved about our little house.

It was only two days later when two of Mary's older sons came to our house. They simply announced that we would move in with them at least for several months until we could adjust to our new life. Mother thanked them but said we would stay in our home and find a way to survive.

The next day, Mary herself came to visit. She reminded us that her husband had died rather suddenly and she remembered the pain that she had suffered. She urged us to come to her house. They had extra room, and fishing families took care of each other. She told us that if we felt we needed to do something, there were things we could do to help in their household. It would not be a burden, and we should come.

Tears welled up in my mother's eyes as she looked at Mary. "You really want us to come live with you?" I will never forget Mary's answer. "No, you are not going to live with us, you are going to be family with us. Please come."

That was a little over four years ago. It was a wonderful blessing. Mother helped with the cooking, and I helped keep the house clean. We were never made to feel like servants. We were family, and we belonged. I didn't think we would ever recover from Father's death, but we did.

Several times in the first two years, my mother talked with Mary about how we should be moving back to our own house and not be a burden to her family. Mary would have nothing to do with such an idea. She told Mother, "You will do no such thing. You are family now, and family members don't just pack up and leave."

It was about three years ago that I met Jesus. Well, I didn't exactly meet him, but that was when he first came to our house. Actually it was Mary's house, but by then, we felt so much at home there that it was "our" house too. Peter came with Jesus, a young teacher from Nazareth. We learned that Peter was going to be working with Jesus on a part-time basis talking about a new life and a new path for Jewish faith.

The next three years were exciting. There were lots of visitors who came whenever Jesus was around. I was never part of the group, but I heard what they talked about, and it was exciting. More and more people were becoming part of a group of followers of Jesus. But then tragedy struck. Jesus was crucified by Rome. You know that story; girls my age were not involved in that story, so I won't say anything about it here.

But the followers of Jesus kept meeting. They felt we had to keep alive what Jesus had taught. We had no idea what lay ahead, but we kept meeting together. James had become the leader of the group, and Peter was a very important member of the leadership team.

Within the first year, we faced several major setbacks. Stephen, a wonderful young man, was killed. Not long after that, Herod killed James, and then one day, Peter was arrested. We were not sure why. That was traumatic. Members of the group met every day to pray that Peter's life might be spared.

A small group was at Mary's house one particular evening praying for Peter when we heard someone at the front gate. I ran to see who was there, knowing I dared not open the gate until I knew exactly who it was. When the voice on the other side said, "Rhoda, it's me, Peter, open the gate," my eyes got big and my mouth dropped wide open. I forgot to open the gate, running back into the house instead, and interrupted the prayer group shouting, "It's Peter! He's at the front gate."

I know I am just a young girl, but I really expected them to believe me. They stopped praying, looked at me, and said, "Don't be crazy! Are you out of your mind?" But I stomped my foot, half jumping up and down, "It is Peter. He's there. I heard his voice." But even that didn't convince anyone. They told me, "It's not Peter. He's in jail. It must be an angel." I thought, *Well, if that's an angel, he sure has Peter's voice.*

Then I heard it again. Peter was still pounding on the front gate, wanting someone to let him in. So I pointed at the gate and said, "Okay. If it's an angel, then who is making all that noise at the front gate?" Finally, one of the men got up, shook his head at me and went to open the gate. As he went, the thought crossed my mind, *You were praying for this! Why don't you expect your prayers to be answered?* But I didn't say anything

Imagine the excitement when he came back with Peter! Everyone was absolutely amazed. He told us how he had escaped from prison. He told us to tell all the others, and he left right away because he knew this would be one of the first places the prison officials would come looking for him.

What a day that turned out to be. We were all so happy to have Peter back again. In all the excitement, I guess people forgot to apologize for not believing me when I had told the truth. I guess I should have opened the gate right away for Peter, but I was so excited to hear his voice I just had to run back inside and tell everyone. It was wonderful news, and I am glad that I was the one who ran to the gate that afternoon. Maybe the next time they will believe me when I tell them something!

—This Rhoda story is in Acts 12:1–17.

48. Take the Risk?

Sometimes, family histories can put pressure on people. Our family was of the tribe of Levi, so we have generations of priestly leadership tucked away in our genealogy. Having once been in the center of religious leadership, our family had difficulty accepting that years ago, grandfather had been quietly pushed out of the temple when the religious climate changed.

I don't know all the details, but our family moved from Jerusalem to the island of Cyprus about two generations before I was born. Most of my life was lived as a Hellenist Jew in the mixed culture setting of Cyprus. That family history shaped my life. We were deeply committed to the Jewish faith, but we had real questions about the direction the religious leadership in Jerusalem was taking the nation.

When I was a young adult, our family moved back to Jerusalem because of economic opportunities, and I became immersed in the religious world without having any official responsibilities.

I saw how the Pharisaic interpretation of the Law limited creativity. I also felt that the Jewish faith of this time period had departed from the life-giving message found in the Mosaic law. I saw the hope for new life with the preaching of John the Baptist, and I very easily fell in step with how the new prophet/teacher Jesus handled the Law. He was saying exactly what I was praying to hear. Jesus had such a positive way of identifying, then contrasting current teachings with what the law of Moses really intended. I knew I had found the Messiah.

My own personal style is to work as a supporting leader from inside the group. I never sought any position of visible leadership, but I invested my life in building networks of relationships, in teaching when asked to explain what Jesus was saying about the Law, about God, and about how we should be living our faith in a new way. My family had believed these things for years, thus it was easy for us to join these informal followers of Jesus.

We suffered the intense pain that everyone in the movement felt when Jesus was crucified. We struggled with what this meant and what we should do. I consider myself very fortunate, because I once was part of a large crowd who saw Jesus after the resurrection. That was enough to tell me that we needed to keep the teachings of this man of God alive because they carried the hope for new life in Judaism and also for the Gentile world.

The first few years were especially difficult. We did not know how Rome would respond to us, so we had to feel our way together. There were several years of famine that presented a major crisis for us because we had many elderly people, widows, and children in this new community. On Cyprus, our family had been very successful economically. For many years, my parents had talked about returning to Jerusalem, and they had made some wise land purchases in anticipation of that return. We were expecting Jesus to return very soon, so it made perfect sense to sell a portion of that land and give the money to the faith community to alleviate the immediate food shortages many were facing.

In the first five years after the death of Jesus, our faith community virtually exploded in number. We had new persons joining us almost every day. This called for more community organization than we had had before, and I was asked to be part of that leadership group. My particular responsibilities emerged over the next year as a teacher for these new members, which also involved integrating them into the fellowship.

There was a problem that was always lurking in the background. A radical member of the Jewish Sanhedrin had vowed to stop the spread of this new faith. He saw it as rejection of the true Jewish faith. He had gained the authority to arrest people simply for wanting to follow Jesus. This forced us to go partially underground in order to save our own lives. There were rumors floating around that he had been converted and had become a follower of Jesus, but most of us did not believe them. We thought that was only a trick to infiltrate our Jesus meetings. But that was three years ago, and there had been no sign of him for those three years.

That is, until the news spread through the church like wildfire: *Paul is back!* Just those words were enough to send a chill through your whole body. We had to be on our guard again, and the tension was high. We were all looking over our shoulders, watching for Paul whenever we met.

I did not know what to think when a Jewish friend who was not a member of our faith came to see me. I knew him as a business friend who was not very religious, so his message had integrity. He told me Paul was back in town. I said I had heard that. Then he asked, "But have you heard the Sanhedrin is very angry with him? He met with a couple of them and told them that they were wrong in what they had done to Jesus and that Jesus was the Messiah." My friend went on to say that Paul wanted to meet with me.

Now that was a challenge. There was no way I wanted to risk meeting Paul. I knew what he had done to some members of our group. But my friend was persuasive. The man really has changed, you have to give him a chance to explain himself. I told him I would think about it, but I made no promises.

What should I do? Should I risk my life? Whom could I believe? I made this a severe matter of prayer, and I kept getting the message, "Barnabas, you have always been a reconciler, a helper, one to reach out to others. You have to meet with Paul or you will never know."

I sent a message through my friend, agreeing to meet with Paul provided he came alone and it was in a very public place. You cannot imagine what was going through my whole body as I walked to that meeting two days later. I could not shake the question, *"Barnabas, are you really ready to die for your faith?"*

Paul and I met. We talked and we talked. Paul told me what had happened to him on the Damascus road, where he had been for the past three years, and how he had gone back through the Scriptures testing everything he had heard that Jesus had said.

He also told me that his wife had left him, all his friends had turned against him, and he had even received few death threats. He asked me to be his friend. Could I help him clean up his reputation in the Jesus community? He had a lot of questions about what Jesus had said, and he wondered where he could get some honest answers. You know, as I listened, I began to like Paul. He was forthright and aggressive, but I sensed a lot of honesty. I knew we could work together.

I promised to see what I could do. Paul and I agreed to meet three days later, and I went back to the leadership of our faith community. Their reaction was definitely not positive. Why had I exposed them to the wrath of Paul the Pharisee? Some were very angry with me. The next day we met again, and I pleaded with them to at least meet with Paul. I had taken that risk, and I was still here. The group looked at each other, and finally, Peter agreed to come with me to meet Paul.

In a very strange way, those two became friends almost immediately. Peter started telling Paul stories about what Jesus had done and said. Paul listened intently, asking a lot of questions, and the conversation went for over two hours.

For the next two weeks, Paul and Peter practically lived together. Peter took Paul to places in Jerusalem where Jesus had healed a person or had talked to the crowd. They even went out to where Jesus was crucified. Peter admitted he had never been back to that terrible place, and it was actually kind of a healing experience to go there. Paul then took Peter to the place just outside the Sanhedrin where Stephen had been stoned to death. Paul went to a spot and just stood there. When Peter looked at him, Paul responded very quietly. "This is where I was standing. And I urged them to throw more stones. I … killed … Stephen."

Peter told me later that Paul tried to fight it, but the tears started to come as he remembered what he had done. Peter said that Paul asked him to forgive him, and that he had gone over to Paul, who was much shorter than Peter, and had held him for a few moments. They cried together over the loss of Peter's friend Stephen.

Those two weeks changed the life of the Jesus community. Paul was accepted, at least by most of us. There were a few who were not ready to forgive him. Peter thanked me often for taking the risk of meeting with Paul. He told me he would not have done it, but he was so glad I had. I appreciated that. I knew Peter had gifts I did not have. It was nice to hear him say that I had gifts he didn't have. I guess that is what it takes to build a vibrant faith community— a recognition of each other's gifts and the encouragement each of us needs to use them.

At the end of the two weeks, we urged Paul to stay, but he said "No". He was going home to Tarsus to be with his family. He wanted time to think; he needed to put his own life back together, which meant he had to find work, probably in his father's tent-making business. Paul was so grateful that he had learned to know us. He asked for forgiveness of almost everyone in the group. It was good to meet the new Paul. Obviously, he was a changed man. I was glad to have him as a brother in the faith.

And then Paul left for Tarsus.

—The Barnabas story is told in Acts 4:36–37, 9:26–27.

49. Don't Kill My Uncle

Growing up in Tarsus was a good experience. It was a multicultural city with Roman politics, Greek culture, and a sizeable minority Jewish population. My grandparents had moved to Tarsus when Rome offered free citizenship for anyone who met certain conditions. You had to be educated and have an occupational skill that would contribute to the expansion of the economy at Tarsus. Grandpa met both of those criteria. He was a devout Jew in the tradition of the Pharisees, and of course Grandma shared those religious views. Grandpa was a leather craftsman who specialized in making tents and awnings.

My mother was older than Uncle Paul, but we always looked up to Paul because we knew he was exceptionally smart and was heading for religious leadership somewhere. My mother had married a Jewish teacher, so education was always important at our house. When my father was offered a teaching position in Jerusalem, there was no question about it; we were going "home" even though neither of my parents had ever lived there.

Only a year or so later, Paul came to live with us as he studied the Torah under Gamaliel. I liked Paul, although I had no interest in becoming a professional religious person.

Even after he got married, Paul was often at our house. He was becoming a very active religious leader, and he took everything so seriously. He talked with my father and me about his concerns for Israel's faith. He was quite upset with a particular Jewish prophet teacher named Jesus who was calling for renewal. Paul had no trouble with the idea of renewal. What made him most angry was this man's rather free and loose interpretation of the Sabbath laws and religious rituals.

I knew Paul was active in a group that was opposed to what this man was teaching, and while I never heard Jesus, I knew that if Uncle Paul didn't like him, I didn't like him either. In many ways, Paul was my idol. I heard the stories about how this radical prophet teacher had been killed by Rome, but we did not talk about that at our house because it was not of any concern to us.

For the next year or so, Paul was actively involved in trying to save the faith by stamping out this dangerous, heretical group. One evening, Paul and his wife came to our house and talked with my parents for a long time. It was quite a tense conversation. Paul had been gone for several days on religious business in Damascus. Something dramatic had happened to him, causing him to go through a radical change in his religious beliefs. My parents clearly sided with Paul's wife and tried to argue with Paul about his betrayal of his faith. When Paul left, it was clear there was a sharp division in the family. That was the last we heard of Paul for several years.

During that time, we stayed in close contact with Paul's wife. She was often in our home talking about what she was going to do. She felt Paul had betrayed her by leaving their Pharisaic faith that had been at the heart of their marriage. She had contacted Paul, telling him that she could not accept his new faith. She could not live with him anymore unless he returned to their common Jewish faith. She told us Paul had responded by saying he did not want her to leave, but if she felt she had to go, she should leave. He was not giving up his new faith in this prophet Jesus, whom he said was the true Jewish Messiah. We heard nothing more from him for several years.

When Paul came back to Jerusalem, he was a changed man with dramatically different religious beliefs that made many Jewish people absolutely furious with him. We had very little contact with him because my parents were not sympathetic with his new religious beliefs. They were clearly upset when he started a riot in the Sanhedrin, with the result that he was being held in the Roman barracks for disturbing the peace. All they told me was that Uncle Paul was being held by Rome.

I missed the way things were before Uncle Paul had changed his religious beliefs. I really liked Paul. He was so intelligent and so enthusiastic about everything he did. I wondered what had gotten him to cause such a dramatic change. But that was Uncle Paul; he would never skip a good argument.

One evening, I was taking a shortcut home, and quite by accident, I heard a group of men talking about killing someone. I was behind some shrubbery so I stopped to hear what they were saying. I could not believe what I was hearing. They were talking about my uncle Paul and how they were going to ambush him in the morning when he returned to meet with the priests and elders at the temple.

When I heard that, I ran. I went directly to the barracks where Paul was being held and told him what I had heard. Paul called a centurion, who took me to the commanding officer. I told him what I had heard the men say. I did not know who they were, but I knew what they had said to each other. Forty men had sworn not to eat or drink until they had killed Paul. My uncle Paul might be wrong in what he believed, but I certainly did not want him to be hurt or worse.

The commanding officer listened very carefully, thanked me for coming, and told me to go home. They would take care of this. But first he ordered me not to tell anyone— emphasis *anyone*—what I had heard.

So I went home. I assumed that anyone included my parents. I knew Mother and Father would be very angry if something happened and they found out I had known about it but had not told them. But I was under Roman orders, so I kept quiet, but I did not sleep very well that night. I worried about Uncle Paul and hoped that nothing bad would happen to him.

—The story of Paul's nephew is in Acts 23:12–35.

50. We Really Didn't Want to Leave

Priscilla and I grew up together in the province of Pontus, just south of the Black sea in northern Asia Minor. We had been friends from childhood and our marriage was a very logical choice. We shared a more progressive understanding of faith.

I grew up in a tent-making family so this became our occupation. Not long after our marriage Priscilla and I accepted an offer by the Roman government for persons with specific occupations to move to Italy in support of their rapid economic growth. It was an opportunity to start our life together in a new setting, and receive Roman citizenship at the same time.

We chose to live in Rome where we were fortunate to arrive at a time when tent-makers were doing quite well financially. We soon developed a reputation for making tents for small merchants who had booths in the village markets.

We were active in one of the synagogues in Rome and for several years this group was our religious community. We had been here almost ten years when we first heard about a prophet-teacher in Palestine. Four persons from our synagogue had been in Jerusalem for Passover. They were present when Peter spoke to a big crowd about Jesus and what he had been teaching. They came home quite excited about everything they had heard. They did not see this as leaving Judaism, it was a new and more inclusive understanding of faith. We talked together a lot, and soon felt it was something we wanted to know more about. This created some tension with the local synagogue leaders, but we remained members as we learned more about Jesus.

Later that summer several followers of Jesus who were living in Antioch were in Rome on business and we met with them. They gave us more information about Jesus and what he had been teaching. We knew the Torah well enough to see how this Jesus was calling for a recovery of the central elements of Jewish faith. Finally, along with several of our friends we left the synagogue to form a small Jesus community in Rome.

Leaving the synagogue created some special problems. We met with the leaders to explain our reasons. We told them we were not leaving Judaism, we simply wanted a more faithful, progressive faith community. One of these meetings exploded because of some very hostile charges made against us. We tried to remain calm, but that was difficult. The synagogue leadership went to the city officials, and accused us of disturbing the peace of Rome. Emperor Claudius was not a very strong leader, and he responded to their pressure by expelling a group of us from Rome. We appealed the decision but Claudius refused to listen. We had to sell everything and leave Rome.

But where should we go? We did not want to return to Pontus, there was no future there. Priscilla and I decided we would go to Corinth. We knew there was a group of Jesus followers there, the economy was good, so that became our destination. Tent-making doesn't require a great deal of equipment, so the move, while inconvenient, was not terribly difficult.

We were warmly welcomed by the Jesus group in Corinth. We were already quite at home when to our great joy, Paul came to our city. We immediately invited him to work with us, since he was an experienced tent maker. He could work during the day and meet at the synagogues with other groups in the evening. We had an extra room in our house so he stayed with us. This was a wonderful opportunity to learn more about our new faith.

Paul stayed with us for several months and we enjoyed working with him at tent-making and in talking with people about Jesus. We were doing well in Corinth. One evening Paul raised a question that created a dilemma for us. He felt it was time for him to move on and he wanted to go to Ephesus. He asked us rather directly; would we consider coming with him to Ephesus for perhaps a year to help form a Jesus group there?

How do you handle that kind of request? We had been expelled from Rome and were doing very well here in Corinth. We had a faith community. We had friends and business was good. It made no sense to leave after only eighteen months. But Paul explained the role we would have. He assured us that we could do tent-making in Ephesus, and that together we would make a good team.

So, we moved again, this time to Ephesus. Once again, we started over with our tent-making business. We easily made connections with other Jewish merchants and their families. We invited people to come listen to Paul talk about Jesus. A little Jesus group formed rather quickly, and new persons were joining every week.

It was inevitable, I guess, that troubles should arise. After Paul left, a Greek speaking Jew from Alexandria, Egypt arrived. Apollos was powerful speaker who had learned a bit about the teachings of Jesus from people in Egypt. But he knew nothing about Pentecost, and relied heavily on the teachings of John the Baptist, interspersed with a few parable sayings from Jesus.

This was troubling for both Priscilla and myself. The man was trying to do the right thing. He knew the Torah well, and he invited people to think about Jesus, but his knowledge was limited to pre-Pentecost information. He knew some things about the teachings of Jesus, but nothing at all about his death and resurrection. It wasn't that he was wrong, he just didn't have the whole story.

Priscilla and I talked much about what to do. Apollos was clearly a much better public speaker than either of us and he had the best of intentions. Who were we to challenge this gifted, sincere, intelligent man?

Finally, we agreed that we had to talk with Apollos. We did not want to be critical, but there was more to the story that he needed to know. It would not be easy, but we did it. We felt very comfortable with this charismatic man. We started by commending him for what he was doing and how he was doing it. When we asked if he knew anything about the resurrection of Jesus, he was quite surprised. He had heard nothing. Would we please tell him about it? He listened with great interest, asking important questions. He thanked us again and again for giving him this new and very important information. From then on, his preaching took on a whole new tone with a far more complete message. We heard from Apollos several times in the next few years as he traveled primarily in Greece. We were glad to hear he was quite successful in telling people the whole story about Jesus.

Things went relatively well for us in Ephesus, but business was much slower and life was hard. One day we learned that the decree which had expelled us from Rome had been withdrawn and we would be welcome to return to the city. This was an easy decision to make. Within a month, Priscilla and I (for the 3rd time) packed our tools, sold our house and moved---this time back to where we had started years ago---in Rome.

When Paul heard about our move, he responded quickly by giving us another job. We were not surprised at that, because Paul had become one of our closest friends. He wrote, describing his dream of going to Spain. He wanted to use us and the Jesus group in Rome as a base for this mission trip to Spain. He acknowledged that he had never been to Rome, and it would be very helpful to have supportive friends when he arrived.

Of course we were delighted, and we told him he would be welcome to stay with us any time. Paul told us that he was writing a very careful letter to the Jesus community in Rome. He wanted to explain his theology in a careful, more systematic way because he was asking for financial support, and it was important that they know what he believed.

Unfortunately, our life in Rome was not what we had hoped it would be. There was significant tension between the new Emperor Nero and the followers of Jesus. Most of the friends we had known ten years ago chose not to return to Rome. It was much harder to make a decent living than it had been in the past, and the faith community seemed to bounce from one problem to another.

After nearly two years we learned that Paul was back in Ephesus, only this time he was in prison. We made the difficult decision that we were needed there to be with Paul as best we could and to help the growing church there. So once again we moved, this time back to Ephesus where we lived for the rest of our lives.

We were not able to help Paul as much as we had hoped. The prison system in Ephesus was not as friendly as in other cities, and not long after we arrived Paul was transferred to Rome. (How is that for unfortunate circumstances). We learned about a year later that our dear friend Paul had been executed by Emperor Nero. It was more than just a personal loss for us, it was a tragedy for the church. Paul was a spirited, bombastic personality, but with his enthusiasm he was able to help a lot of people. We ourselves owed him so much. We were blessed to have known him so intimately. We had so much for which we were thankful, yet the death of Paul stayed with us for the rest of our lives. A friend like Paul is not easily forgotten.

The Aquila and Priscilla story is in Acts 18.

51. I Can Tell a Good Story

I was an innocent little girl who had done absolutely nothing wrong. Why pick on me just because my country lost a war with Rome? I played no part in that war, yet my father was killed, and I was taken captive when I was only twelve.

I was taken from my home near Babylon by slave traders who forced us to walk—while they rode camels—all the way from Babylon to Antioch, nearly five hundred miles. Every step of the way, I learned to hate these people even more. I was a child, and they didn't seem to care whether I lived or died. I stayed alive by making up stories as we walked. I made up a story about every person or thing we passed. But I never told anyone; I kept them all to myself.

When we got to Antioch, we were put on a ship for Athens. If I thought that walking across the desert was bad, the seven days in the hold of that ship were far worse. At least in the desert there was a wind blowing and you could see the sun during the day and the stars at night. That helped you think that maybe somewhere, up there in the stars, there were some gods who at least knew where you were.

But in the ship there was no breeze, no sun, no stars. People were crammed so tightly together that you could hardly breathe, and when you did breathe, you really didn't want to because the stench was sickening. People died on that boat, and we could not even throw their bodies overboard. We literally had to take turns sleeping because we could not all lie down at the same time. Going hungry was better than eating the awful food they fed us.

Landing in Athens was a blessing. I and about a dozen other girls my age were taken to a prison for several days, where I was given sort of decent food and was allowed to wash. I was given a new (well not new, but it was new for me) dress. I didn't know what was going to happen, but it could not have been worse than what had already happened.

Then we were told we were going to be taken to the slave market that afternoon, and we should be on our best behavior because if we looked good and behaved, we would bring more money and people might actually want us. I think that was supposed to make us feel good, but the thought of being a slave for the rest of my life was not good news. They might want me, but I knew I did not want them.

Standing in that slave market was the most embarrassing thing I had ever experienced. Back home I was a good child. I had been raised in a good home. I knew what was right and proper, how to behave, and how to dress. When we got to the slave market, they simply tore our clothes off, and we were forced up on this stage naked—right in front of everybody. If I could have, I would have killed that slave trader right on the spot. But when your hands are tied and your feet are loosely roped together, and you are only twelve you can't do much to defend yourself.

I thought to myself, *"Okay, my best hope is to get the attention of some rich family who will treat me better than just any old man."* So I cheered up as best I could and looked as bright eyed as possible. It worked. A well-dressed man with a woman standing beside him began to bid on me. I was pleased with myself because I didn't go cheap. I thought that was a positive sign.

I was taken to the small city of Philippi, way up north from Athens. My new owners were business people, and they put me to work as a house servant. Other than the fact that I was still a slave, it wasn't that bad. For the first year, I listened and learned the language and did what I was told. There were small children in this household, and I had great fun telling them stories. Those days in the desert were paying off. I passed my time working in the master's house and telling stories to the younger children.

One evening, we had a big dinner with lots of guests, and my owner called for me to come in and tell some stories to our guests. I told stories like the ones I had made up out in the desert, only I made them more creative and more dramatic.

The next week my master took me out to the town square, where he made me tell more stories, and I began to create stories about how the gods in the heavens came down and did things to people. I had seen enough of what people did to other people, so it wasn't hard to imagine what the gods would do.

That began to be my work. I would sit in the town square and tell stories. One day, a rich-looking man came up and asked me what I thought the gods would do to him. I thought for a moment and made up a story about how the gods liked him and wanted to be good to him. He liked that and gave me some money (which my master immediately took from me!)

More and more often I began mixing storytelling with fortune-telling. They really aren't that different. I developed the skill of looking at a person and creating a story almost immediately. If they were well dressed and looked rich, I told a good story. If they were ugly and dirty, I said the gods were evil and they would suffer. I don't know how much money I made because my owners took it from me right away, but they made me work out there every day. And the worse the stories that I told about what the gods might do, the more they liked it.

One day, a group of men from out of town walked past me. I could tell they were foreign by the way they were dressed and their accent as they talked. I decided I had nothing to lose, so I began telling a story about them and how they were gods come to save us all from our sins and how they would do terrible things to us if we didn't listen. Every day, I made the story a little bit worse. They would walk past me trying to ignore me, but I would follow them for a few minutes, telling all who were listening about what terrible things these people would do.

On the fourth day, one of the men turned around, walked right up to me, and said rather loudly, "That's enough. Stop it right now. Stop doing this to people." I stopped and looked up at him, bewildered by his response. He lowered his voice and talked directly to me. "You don't have to do this anymore. You are hurting people by what you say, just as you were hurt by what people did to you. You are better than that. Don't hurt other people just because they hurt you. Tell your master I took away your power. Tell him you can't help it you don't have that power any more. He won't hurt you."

And with that he turned and walked away. I looked at him as he left, and suddenly, I wasn't angry any more. I had never wanted to make other people suffer; I had just never thought about it. I stood there for a minute, then slowly turned and walked home.

That evening, I told my master what had happened and how the gift of fortune-telling was gone—I just didn't have it any more. I was so scared. Fourteen-year-old slave girls aren't supposed to talk to their owners like that.

Well, he got angry all right, but not at me. He swore he would get that man for doing this. I don't know what he did or whether it worked, but he never took it out on me. I still told stories to the children, but I never did fortune-telling again. I heard my master was telling people I'd had a demon that had made me tell these stories but the demon was gone, so I couldn't do it anymore. I didn't know anything about demons, and I didn't think I ever had one, but if that solved the problem for my master, I guess it was okay with me.

—This story is told in Acts 16:16–18, but the story for Paul goes through verse 40.

52. Generosity on Display

We both came from business families. When we were married my parents gave us some land a short distance outside Jerusalem. They promised that when they died, since I was an only child, we would receive the remainder of the family property. They knew that Ananias had a strong background in olive orchards and vegetable farming. This was their way of affirming our marriage.

Ananias and I were both raised in active religious Jewish families, and we observed all the traditional Jewish practices of letting portions of our property lie fallow each year, giving the local poor access to fruit and vegetables on that land. We both believed that God honored this practice, and we were quite successful in our orchard and vegetable farming.

The one thing that was a disappointment for us was that we had no children. We had done the best we could, but that never happened. We decided we would not be bitter but would dedicate a small percentage of the money we made to support the temple ministry of caring for orphan children.

When my parents died, we received the family inheritance as promised, and our farm more than doubled in size. About this same time, some of our friends were fascinated with a young prophet teacher who was traveling around the countryside. We were both of the Sadducee tradition in Jewish faith, and our friends told us that we would agree with much of what this young teacher was saying about the law.

We went to hear him several times and found much to our delight, that we heard a positive message about Judaism's future. We liked his message about living together in God's new way and not allowing Rome to dictate our beliefs. We liked his concern for children, for women, and for the poor. We had worked at those issues for all our married life.

So we began supporting his ministry. At that time, we did not join anything because there was no organization to join. But we felt good about being part of something we believed had a future.

Then there was that terrible Passover weekend. But you know that story, so I won't repeat it here. It was an unbelievably painful time. People who had been following Jesus began to meet to work through their grief and talk about how they could keep the Jesus vision for a new world alive. Over the next year, the group literally exploded in size. Those were very exciting days for us all.

But as with any infant organization, problems arose. Tensions developed between our group and the traditional Jewish religious leaders. They retaliated by removing those widows and orphans who were followers of Jesus from the temple food ministry. The Jewish system had worked very well. To be removed from that list created a distinct hardship for many, so the leaders of our new community met and decided we would take over this ministry. For us personally, this was a simple matter; we just transferred what we had been giving to the temple for widows and orphans to the new Jesus organization, and that worked quite well.

There was a technicality that did trouble us a bit, however. Most of the people in the new Jesus community had very little property. Gradually, people began turning their property over to the group to avoid having it seized by Jewish authorities. This way, they could honestly say it wasn't really their property. In exchange for the property, the leaders of the new Jesus movement promised to take care of the people who had given property for as long as they lived. But we had substantial property; that was how we made our living, and it was from this property that we could give generously to the movement. We did not feel that we could do that with our own property.

However, we saw an interesting dynamic developing within the group. People were proving their commitment by turning over their houses or their garden plots to group ownership. This gave them status, and they were praised by the community for their acts of faith.

Our good friend Barnabas, a truly good man, sold some land he owned and turned over a large sum to the group. The group needed the money, but we were concerned about what we would do if the money ran out and no one had any more land to give.

So Ananias and I did some careful financial planning. There was a section of land on the edge of our property that for the last year we had been talking about selling because we wanted to make some improvements in our warehouses and in our own house. We agreed that we would sell the land and give some of the proceeds to the new community. But we also felt we needed to keep some of the income from this sale to make the improvements needed on the rest of the property.

Also, we had no children who would take care of us in our old age. We weren't absolutely positive that the new intentional community would have the financial resources in ten years to take care of everyone as they were promising. We felt it only right that we guaranteed the stability of our future and not be completely at the mercy of the community. We were getting up in years, and Ananias's health had not been the best this past year. We worried about that.

We sold the land, keeping about a third to ensure our future, and Ananias took the rest to the apostles as our contribution and commitment to the group. It was a large sum of money, and we felt we were being quite generous.

—Here I am going to let Peter take over the story—you'll understand why!

I was surprised when Ananias brought this large gift to the community. He told me that he and Sapphira had decided this was their faith community and they wanted to be fully part of it. I saw the amount and knew something about their farm, so I asked, "Is this all you got for your land?" I knew him to be a better businessman than that. He told me that was it, and they would have to trust the community like everyone else. I challenged him at that point, because I was sure he was lying. I felt that lying was the quickest way to destroy community life that there is. And I told him he was lying to us and to God.

I knew Ananias was not in the best of health, but I did not expect him to have a heart attack and die right in front of me. But that is what happened.

A couple hours later, Sapphira came in, asking if Ananias had been there, because he had not come home. I asked her about the money, and she told me the same lie Ananias had told us. I said to her, "Sapphira, you are lying. Ananias was here, told us the same lie, and when we told him that he was sinning against God, he had a heart attack and died right here in this room. And you are guilty of the very same thing."

Sapphira was visibly shocked. Without a word, she turned and walked away. In less than a month she also died! It was a major blow to the community, but it did teach us a lesson in honesty and generosity before God.

—The Ananias and Sapphira story is in Acts 5.

53. I Changed My Mind

My life started out badly. My mother did not know who my father was. She tried to raise me as best she could, but single mothers were not well respected in Rome. We lived in the ghetto in south Rome, where survival was always a challenge. I went to school when I could, but I wasn't a good student, so that wasn't a high priority for me, and my mother was not around to discipline or encourage me.

When I was about sixteen, my mother simply disappeared, and suddenly I was on my own. I learned months later that she had been killed by an angry "client," and in her line of work, identification was not expected, so no one knew who she was. Her body was simply disposed of by the authorities.

That forced me to make my own decisions, so joining the army was an easy thing to do. It promised security, food, and a place to live. As a soldier, I was part of a group for the first time in my life. I developed self-confidence and was determined to prove myself in the Roman army.

One of the advantages was that I got to travel. My legion fought in Europe, Africa, and Syria. Once, we were stationed in Greece for two years, and during this time I met a woman who agreed to marry me. Both of us came from unfortunate family situations, and we knew the odds, but we were determined to make it work. She remained in Greece, and I was home with her for a portion of each year. In the next five years, we had two children.

I wanted to be a good father, so as soon as I was eligible, I applied for promotion to centurion. This would provide a more stationary position, and we could be a legitimate family. But I was passed over for undisclosed reasons.

Two years later, I applied again, and again I was passed over. This time I got the message. Being passed over twice was a certain indication I would never be promoted beyond my current legionnaire status.

That was more than discouraging. It meant I would spend the rest of my life being a soldier, forever on active duty at a moment's notice. That is when I heard that the city of Philippi was looking for a jailer. You need to understand a couple of things about jailers. Being a jailer is a military position. But soldiers on the way up do not apply to be jailers because it is a dead-end occupation. The pay is abysmal, and nobody wants to a friend of the jailer.

But my wife argued that it meant a stable place to live and assurance that we would be together. That would mean that the children would have a father. So I applied, was accepted, and we moved to Philippi.

Being the jailer at Philippi was actually not that bad. We never had hardened criminals, mostly petty thieves, drunks, and people who had committed other relatively minor offenses. Roman jails had an excellent record for security. People did not escape from a Roman jail. It was several months after beginning my work at Philippi that I found out why. Regulations are that if a prisoner escapes from a jail, the jailer is required to serve out the remainder of that prisoner's sentence. That is good motivation for the jailer to discourage attempts at escaping.

That evening, there was nothing unusual about getting two men for disturbing the peace. It happened all the time. These two were from Jerusalem, so I assumed they were Jewish. I put them in one of the inner security cells and followed standard procedure of putting locks and chains on their ankles. They didn't look like they would be a problem, but I was taking no chances.

Our house was connected to the jail, and around midnight, I heard noises coming from the jail. I wasn't especially concerned because that often happened. But I checked it out and found these two Jewish men were singing and praying and talking to the other prisoners. Most prisoners do not sing while in jail, but they were singing Jewish religious songs. I had heard them years ago when I was stationed in Israel, so I went back home to bed.

I was just crawling into bed when I felt the house shake. Earthquakes were rare, but we had had tremors before in Philippi. But this one was no minor tremor; it was a big one, enough to make the whole house shake. That got my attention, and I quickly got dressed and went back over to the jail to make sure everyone was safe.

What I found was a jailer's absolute worst nightmare. The cell doors were standing open. The chains had come out of the walls. The place was a mess with no security anywhere. I knew the regulations. Given the population of the jail that night, I would be spending the next 30 to 40 years in my own prison. That would be for the rest of my life. I knew what other jailers had done in this kind of situation. I reached for my sword. I was not going to live the rest of my life as a prisoner in my own jail.

But then I heard a loud voice. "Don't do that! We are all here. Nobody has left." I opened my eyes, grabbed a torch, and did a quick survey. We had five men serving ten-year sentences who were all sitting in their cells, or what used to be their cells. All the other prisoners were there. All of Them!! Unbelievable!

I stepped inside one of the cells and asked, "What is going on here?" One of the long-term prisoners said, "We were listening to these two guys from Jerusalem. They were telling us about their religious beliefs, talking about justice, and what God wants from each of us. When the place collapsed, they right away told us not to run because we would get caught and almost certainly would be killed. They had been in jails before and they know the system. We don't like it here, but as least we know in four or five years we will get out. That is better than being hunted down and killed. So here we are!"

Then I turned to the two men, Paul and Silas, and asked them, "What kind of religious faith do you have? It sounds different from any religion I've ever heard about." Right then, some other guards and jail officials began showing up, expecting the worst. I told them everyone was here although the place was a mess. I said I wanted everyone cleaned up and fed before transferring them to another jail. And I did not want *any* rough treatment of anyone. I assured the prisoners that as soon as this place was repaired, they would be brought back here, and I would see that they got good treatment because they had stayed when they could have run away. I owed them that.

When things calmed down and everyone was taken care of, I took Paul and Silas to my house. I told them I wanted to know more about their religion. I had never been a religious person, but I did care about people. My wife and I remembered the hardships of our childhood, and we wanted better for our own children. I wanted to know what I had to do to have this salvation they were talking about.

We got some food and listened to their story. My wife and I were both excited about they told us. This group had something that we never had, and the more they talked, the more we knew we wanted it. They explained that they had a ritual that they used to include people in their religious group, so we were both "baptized" on the spot.

They also told us that there was a group of Jesus followers who met regularly in the city and that we would be welcome to join this group. I doubted that and told Paul I did not believe him. I was a jailer. No one wants to be friends with me. He assured me that his group was different. He promised that he and Silas would introduce us to some of the members and that we would be warmly accepted.

I looked at my wife, and she was crying. Between her tears, she managed to say, "You mean we can have some friends, friends who have children who will play with our children?"

That day, salvation truly came to our house.

—The story of the Philippian jailor is in Acts 16:25-34

54. From Thief to Bishop in the Church

I was at work, doing my job keeping records for a small company. My parents were professional people with some private resources, and I had received a good education. Rome had invaded my country and had quickly occupied our tiny nation. But our small town had avoided any direct military activity. We had settled back into a normal routine when a Roman legion came into town one day and seized about twenty young men and women. We had no warning and absolutely no chance to resist or even flee. We were simply carried off by the army with no opportunity to say good-bye to parents or friends and no idea where we were being taken. I learned later that was just how Rome did it. Your future was taken from you, and in the space of a few minutes you had become a slave. The sad thing was there was virtually nothing you could do about it. To your family, it was as though you were dead.

I was taken about two hundred miles away and sold at a slave auction. It was so unfair, and I was so angry, but when you are in chains with Roman soldiers all around, any resistance would get you killed.

I must admit, given the situation, I was fortunate. A wealthy Greek businessman bought me, and I became the accountant and business manager for his company. I was back doing what I had been trained to do. I was not mistreated physically, and I had decent living quarters with good food. But I was a slave. I had no freedom, and I was expected to work long hours every day. This was now my life, but I was determined almost immediately that I was not going to do this for the rest of my life.

You need to understand that in the Roman Empire, being a slave meant you were no longer a person, you were property. You had no rights, no freedom. If you tried to run away, the army would come after you. They would return you to your owner, and then in front of everyone, they would kill you as a way of teaching other slaves not to run away. It was an effective method of slave control.

But there was another way, one that was not available to most slaves. If you could get the money, you could buy your freedom. I was the accountant, the manager, and I paid the bills for my owner's company. I knew I had to be careful, but I also knew how it could be done. Four of us set up a foolproof system to overpay bills and receive regular dividend payments from the billing company. It took careful record keeping, but for five years we were making it work. That is until one day when one of others made a mistake and got caught. I knew it would only be a day or two until everything would fall apart for me.

I told Philemon, my owner, that I had to go to Ephesus, one day away, to clear up a problem with a company that had overcharged us. He agreed. That evening, I took all the money I had saved plus some new identity documents I had created and I ran. I knew it was risky, but I also knew how to do it right. Most runaway slaves tried to return home, and that was exactly where owners went to look for them. I, however, headed for Rome with money and a new identity. No one would ever look for me there.

I had been in Rome for almost a month when quite by accident I heard a Jewish preacher talking about freedom, about forgiveness, and mercy, plus a whole new way of living. I knew that was what I wanted, so I went back the next day and again on the third day to hear him. I stayed on the third day and talked with the man they called Paul. I learned he was a trained Jewish rabbi and a member of a new religious community who were followers of Jesus. That did not mean anything to me except that I liked the philosophy behind what Paul was saying. I explained to him that I was trained in writing and accounting and that I could be a lot of help to him. He immediately agreed, and I went to work for Paul.

I learned right away that he was awaiting trial for his religious beliefs and that he was under semi-official Roman control. That was an excellent cover for me. I had some resources and I had official papers that only a legal expert would have found problems with. I worked with Paul, making arrangements, handling his money, writing letters, anything he wanted done. I also began to believe that Paul's religious beliefs matched what I wanted for my life, and I became a "follower" with Paul in this new way taught by Jesus.

For over a year this arrangement was perfect. I felt safe, I had work, I was making new friends, and my past was gone. I had literally become a new man. I knew that finally I was truly free. But then one day, with a single piece of papyrus, my world fell apart.

Paul got a letter, and he was very excited. He told me that an old friend Epaphras was coming from Laodicea to visit, and he knew we would become good friends. That letter signaled the end for me. The coming of Epaphras made everything different. You see, I knew Epaphras. And worse yet, Epaphras knew me. He was a close friend and business associate with Philemon, my former owner. It was one of Epaphras's slaves who got caught in our old slave group back at Laodicea two years ago.

I didn't know what to do, so I decided to take what I had and run away again. Paul heard me leaving and demanded to know what was going on. Have you ever had to tell the best friend you ever had that you are a liar, a cheat, a thief, and a runaway slave? That is when Paul quietly reminded me that what I had done made him guilty of harboring a runaway slave and thus I had put a death penalty on his head too! I wanted to die. How could I have done that to him?

Paul and I spent the rest of the night arguing about what I was going to do. He argued that the only chance either of us had was to write a letter to Philemon and ask Epaphras to serve as our personal ambassador with Philemon. I argued that if I just left, Epaphras would never need to know I'd ever been there, and everything would be all right with Paul. But as I said, Paul was very persuasive. Get him in an argument and he was tenacious.

Epaphras arrived two days later, and was he ever furious when he saw me. We had to physically restrain him from calling the Roman guards on the spot. It took Paul a week to convince him to plead our case with Philemon. That was the worst week of my life. I couldn't eat, I couldn't sleep. All I could think about was running away, but Paul would hear nothing of it.

Paul worked for days on that letter. We wrote and then rewrote sentences, changed words, restating what we wanted. It is hard to write a letter when your life depends on your ability to say it exactly right.

Finally, Epaphras and I left Paul and headed for Laodicea. I still did not want to go. Do you enjoy being forced to face up to the mistakes you have made? How can you look forward to going home when you know your death is a distinct possibility? Paul kept insisting that everything would be alright, that I should trust God. But believe me, trusting God can be very hard to do sometimes.

When we got to Laodicea, Epaphras told me to stay out of sight while he met with Philemon. That meeting took forever. I could hear Philemon arguing with Epaphras. Finally, Epaphras came out and told me to go in, that Philemon had promised to listen to me tell my story.

I was trembling all over as I confessed what I had done, how I had gone to Rome, had met Paul, and had become a follower of Jesus. I talked about my commitment to Paul and what I had been doing as Paul's personal assistant. Philemon listened without saying a word. When I finished, the only thing I could do was look at him. Then Philemon slowly got up, came over to me, extended his hand, pulled me to my feet, and embraced me. As he held me, he said, "I should be very angry with you, but I trust Paul, and as I hear what you have done with your life, I forgive you. I promise to accept you as a follower of Jesus with me. Welcome home, Onesimus."

We both just stood there for more than a moment. My whole body shook as I sobbed on his shoulder, and I could feel Philemon's tears on my own neck. I vowed in that moment that I would live my life in gratitude for the forgiveness I had just experienced.

For the next three years, I worked with Philemon. I didn't have my old job, but he gave me responsibility to supervise the slaves who worked in his company. He also encouraged me to reflect on what I had learned from Paul. I had an opportunity to spend significant time with Peter and Mark to hear their stories. I even went to Antioch and then to Jerusalem, meeting with the leaders of the Jesus movement. The acceptance I received and the trust they showed in me was most gratifying as I told my story, honestly and openly.

Unfortunately, it was only a few years later that Paul and Peter were killed by Nero in Rome. It was a devastating loss for the church. Several leaders from Ephesus came to me, asking if I would give leadership to the emerging faith community not as a pastor but as an administrator, helping the various groups stay connected with each other.

Philemon said I should go with his blessing, so I did. It was a task I thoroughly loved—meeting with people, encouraging them to share their faith stories with each other, and finding ways to be helpful as we struggled to shape our identity. I had really just begun to see the results of my work when leaders from several other faith communities in the region asked if I would include their congregations in my oversight work.

It was then that I discovered that some of these churches had received letters from Paul offering counsel and guidance in congregational life. That gave me the vision of trying to collect all the letters of Paul that I could find, and to bring them together in one place making them available for all the churches in the region. I felt I owed that to Paul for what he had done for me.

I was able to gather six letters. As I read through them, I had the powerful feeling that one important letter was missing. I went back to Philemon, now an old man, and asked for the letter Paul had written to him on my behalf. Philemon did not want to give it to me. He felt that the very effective work I was doing in the church would be damaged if people who did not know me found out that I had once been a runaway slave who had stolen money. He urged me to keep that bit of history in the past; no one needed to know that.

We had a long talk. I explained to Philemon that people needed to know the power of forgiveness, even church leaders have a history, and God forgives and offers new life. If I could continue to tell my story honestly and openly, perhaps other people would experience the same forgiveness you offered to me. And I asked again, "May I have the letter to include in the collection of Paul's letters that we are circulating in the churches of the area?"

This time Philemon said yes. He acknowledged that when I came back with Epaphras that day years ago, he was determined to make me pay dearly for what I had done. But Paul's letter, with Epaphras's urging, and then hearing my own story had convinced him to forgive me. He told me, "It had to be God's doing, because it was not what I had intended. But I have never been sorry I did it. You have been a blessing to me and to the church. What a tragedy it would have been if I had stood in the way of God that afternoon so many years ago. Here is the letter with my blessing."

The book of Philemon is the letter written by Paul on behalf of Onesimus.

List of Persons

Scripture References

References Refer to Story Number(s)

Matthew

1:18–2:15	1, 2, 3
2:1–12	8
8:28–34	22
9:1–8	23
9:18–26	30
10:4	37
12:9–14	24
14:13–21	32
15:21–28	13
20:29–34	19
21:10–17	34
22:3–6	38
23:31–43	39
23:50–56	40
24:13–35	43
26:6–13	35
26:14–16	37
26:47–56	37
27:57–61	39
27:62–28:15	40

Luke

1:5–25, 57–80	10
1:26–2:20	1, 2
2:6-7	6
2:8–20	8
2:36–38	9
2:41-52	33
5:17–26	23
6:6-11	24
7:11–17	18
7:36–50	35
8:26–39	23
8:34-43	12
8:40–56	13, 30
9:10–17	32
9:49–50	26
10:38–42	15,16
12:13–22	31
17:11–19	20
19:1–10	25
23;32-43	38
24:13-35	42
25:50-60	39

Benton Mennonite Church
15350 County Road 44
Goshen, Indiana 46528

CPSIA information can be obtained at www.ICGtesting.com
Printed in the USA
LVOW07s0714260515

439552LV00001B/2/P